PRAISE FOR *DOMINATE THE TOP*

Jeffrey Kirk has done it again. For years Jeff has been my go-to man when I need advice on SEO or SEM.

Through **Dominate The Top**, Jeff takes the complex issues small business owners face in competing online, and he navigates us step-by-step to success in greater search engine positioning, getting our websites noticed, and driving the results we want.

If you want to crush your competition and dominate the top... this book is for you.

– Bryan-David Scott
Celebrity Coffee Chef
Luxury Coffee Specialist at Cup of Luxury

What I like best about Jeffrey Kirk, and now his new book, **Dominate the Top** is how he simplifies the learning and the doing.

Jeffrey's newest book makes the phrase "how to" really easy. I believe this book is what we all need when it comes to developing our websites, marketing, and being found through the internet.

This is a must read. Use it as a road map in helping you build your online marketing plans.

– Larry S. Cockerel
National Sales Training Specialist
Author and International Leadership Speaker
Trainer with the John C. Maxwell Team

Very interesting and informative. Though I am not a website developer, I felt compelled to put all these new discoveries into practice right away.

In this book, Jeffrey Kirk made it all so simple that I felt there was nothing holding me back. Now I can't wait to get the workbook!

– Mike Theisen
Director of Marketing at Liberty Dance Center
Volunteer Coach/Mentor at SCORE

An invaluable resource for businesses that want to have a greater online presence. If you take the time to follow the recommendations presented in this book, expect to see results. Our company's website traffic has grown by 81.86% in just one month!

– Jenna Dehn
Office Manager and Marketing Support at Armitage Research

Dominate The Top

Dominate The Top

Simple Website Fixes to Rise in the Search Results and Crush Your Competition

JEFFREY KIRK

Dominate the Top
**Simple Website Fixes to Rise in the Search Results
and Crush Your Competition**

Disclaimers:
This book is for educational purposes only. While every attempt has been made to verify the information provided herein, the author does not assume any responsibility for errors, omissions, or inaccuracies. Because of the dynamic nature of the Internet, any web addresses or links contained in this book may have changed since publication and may no longer be valid.

Furthermore, the advice, strategies, and opinions expressed herein may not be appropriate for every situation or business. Additionally, there is no way for the publisher or author to know the present state of your business, or website, or your capacity to implement the recommendations provided. Therefore we cannot, and do not, guarantee or imply that you will achieve any particular results. Neither the publisher nor the author shall be liable for any loss of profit or any other commercial damages, including but not limited to direct, indirect, general, special, incidental, exemplary, consequential, or other damages.

Published by:

Up At Dawn Publishing
2824 North Burton Court
Waukesha, WI 53188

www.upatdawn.biz

ISBN-13: 978-0-692-32392-2 (paperback)

Printed in the United States of America

Up At Dawn Publishing Revision Date: 15-May-2015

For Bryn,
whom God put in my world
to share my world
and brighten my world!

TABLE OF CONTENTS

PREFACE

My journey into the internet began more than 20 years ago, back in early 1993, with my first "ecommerce" business. Certainly I have to use the term ecommerce a bit loosely. We didn't call it ecommerce back then. My company was called Omni International Trading Company, and I sourced goods from around the world and delivered them into Kazakhstan, one of the countries of the former Soviet Union.

To get the products I was looking for, I used computer networks such as CompuServe and the World Trade Center network. I also used a fax machine.

My business partner in Kazakhstan and I were 12 time zones apart. Finding time to talk on the phone, and getting a suitable connection, was difficult and expensive. Trading faxes was also problematic since doing so relied on a clean phone connection that spanned half the world.

So in 1993, I bought a modem for my partner, and subscribed to a Moscow-based internet service for his use. When I visited him, I installed the modem and the software, and showed him how to send and receive email.

Now we had a competitive advantage. He could compose a message for me and then connect to a phone system only 1,300 miles away. Yeah, that's still long distance, but much closer than the 5,600 miles (as the crow flies) between us (assuming a crow would actually fly the shortest route, directly over the top of the earth).

The nice thing was that once he successfully connected to his internet provider, the message came to me exactly as intended. I could read, take whatever action, and respond. At his next convenience he would get my message.

What I found in this process was that the internet could be quite useful for business. That understanding moved me to start a new business in 1995, providing internet access and website design in my local community.

I'll be the first to admit that back when I got started, I was more of a tech geek. The technology was cool: routers, servers, T1 lines, operating systems, programming languages, and how it all fit together. I didn't really know anything about marketing. I didn't really know much about running a business either.

To go back nearly a decade prior to that point, I had studied computer science and math in college and went on to become employed as a software engineer with a good career ahead of me. But, led by entrepreneurial desires, I dove into the idea of starting my own business and left my software engineering position at the beginning of 1993 for a world of unknowns.

Within a couple years, as I started creating websites for businesses, I quickly learned that just because you build it, does not mean that anyone will come. The secret sauce, I came to find out, was marketing. But I had not been trained in marketing. And I didn't think I really knew all that much about it either.

Even as recently as 8 or 9 years ago, I still thought that successful marketing required some special knowledge or skills that I didn't possess. I could guess at an approach and get it right sometimes, but not all the time.

And then I met Brad Sugars, founder of Action Coach, the largest business coaching company in the world. And Brad said one thing that connected all the dots for me. He said, "Marketing is math." Seriously? That's all? Then the logic fell into place for me. "If marketing is math, and I am good at math, then it follows that I am good at marketing."

You see, when I discovered that I could make an educated guess and get it right some of the time, that's actually a good starting point. No one gets it right all of the time. The factor that improves the results is the testing. Take good guesses and test them against each other, distilling the results down to numbers. Once the numbers work, so does the marketing.

Of course I understand that in practice marketing is more than math alone. There are proven strategies. There is human psychology. There are the 4 P's - price, product, promotion, and place. There are many factors you can consider, but the part that makes it all work is the math. You must have the ability to compare the results of two or more tests to determine which produced the greatest success. Because when you can prove it, you can constantly improve it for better and better results.

There are many different things that can be tested. When considering websites, one of the elements that can make a profound difference is the copy, i.e. the text on a page. Even this is an over-generalization, as there are different parts within the text of a website which can be modified and tested independently. In the chapters that follow you will see many examples of how words make a difference.

To put the importance of copywriting into a brief nugget of truth, I will quote David Deutsch. I took a copywriting course from him in 2008 and had the good fortune to interview him in an internet marketing training series called the "Web Genius Summit" that I hosted back in 2010. In that interview, David said this:

"Copywriting is really just the whole way that your business interfaces with the rest of the world. And if that's not optimum, then everything else is obscured.

"It's like a windowpane. If you're a storekeeper and your front window is dirty and you can't see anything through it, it affects your whole business. And it's the same with copywriting."

So now how do we apply all this for your benefit? The concepts presented in this book are rather simple. Some are common sense. Yet, for some reason, many are missed in the development of business websites. Many businesses fail to have effective websites because of the common belief that websites are technology projects. Website development is often treated like buying a new computer network rather than being looked at as a marketing campaign.

What I am presenting here is not rocket science. It's not even math. Though I brought up math, and made the connection with marketing, most of this book will not look at the math. There are things you can improve even before the numbers come into play. But before you get to the end of this book, I will show you some simple ways to look at the numbers. The best part, in this case, is that the calculations are all done for you!

In the end, the only thing that really matters are your results.

IMPROVE YOUR RESULTS – GET THE WORKBOOK

Some readers have expressed interest in having a workbook to accompany the material in this book. This way they can have their notes and action steps in one place.

If you would like a workbook to help you get better and faster results, there is one available to you. You can get more details, and download your own copy from here:

www.dominatethetop.com/workbook

INTRODUCTION

When your potential customers and clients are sitting in front of the empty Google search box, you are hoping they find your business.

Google is the most-used search engine in the world, so you're pretty sure that a large number of your prospects are using this tool. Since that's the case, you need to work with Google to move ahead of your competition.

In order to appear on the first page of Google results you have to give Google what they want, what they care about most.

But what is that?

Keep in mind that Google's business model is to create a great user experience. That means they want to send visitors to exactly the website that fulfills their search request.

If someone clicks on a search result and 5 seconds later is back at Google doing another search, Google failed to deliver.

Consider this: If 100% of the time that you did a search, you got exactly what you wanted, wouldn't you always use that search provider?

That's what Google wants you to do. Therefore hitting that 100% target is their goal. So, how can they best deliver on these user experience goals? What factors do they have to consider as quality indicators?

That's what they care about. And, for our purposes, there are 3 things we need to consider. Those top 3 things are Uniqueness, Relevancy, and Popularity. Very briefly, I'll define each of these terms.

Uniqueness is about the content, mostly the words, on your website. You can easily imagine this is important if you consider what would happen if there were little uniqueness among websites. What if there were 1,000 identical websites in response to your search? What would Google display? They could just as well present the sites to you randomly. You don't want your site mixed in with 1,000 identical sites. So it's good for you to know that you control uniqueness—100%.

Relevancy is the relationship between your site and the search words chosen. In other words the closer your site matches the topic searched, the more relevant your site is for those search results. By choosing how you present your uniqueness, you can have a large impact on relevancy.

Popularity is not so much in your control. It is very subjective and it tries to answer the question, "Do people really care about what your site has to say?" If nobody cares then there's no point in displaying your website, even if it is unique and relevant. But if people like to visit and use your site, then it demonstrates popularity, and it can win out over less popular sites.

There's more to each of these, but if you understand those concepts then you have a pretty good basis to make improvements.

By now you have probably probably heard of what I like to call the Google Zoo. The zoo contains types of animals such as Panda, Penguin, and Hummingbird. Each of these is a code word for a significant change in Google's search algorithm. The details of the algorithms are more or less secret, but the overriding impact is not.

Each time Google makes an algorithmic adjustment, they are attempting to get closer to their goal of total search perfection. To do that, they are adjusting various factors related to uniqueness, relevancy, and popularity.

No one knows more about human activity on the internet than Google does. They can use this vast data to judge the searcher's intent in an attempt to provide the exact information that is desired on any given search. As more people come online to do searches, and as more services become available, the importance of some of the data shifts. Google can take advantage of that new knowledge to produce better and better results.

In order to create the greatest chance of getting your site seen in Google search results, you want to work on all three of these major factors. But that's too much to include in a single book.

I actually want to take you one step back from looking at Uniqueness, Relevancy, and Popularity and focus on one key sentence from above:

If someone clicks on a search result and 5 seconds later is back at Google doing another search, Google failed to deliver.

That is Google's perspective. If someone bounces back to search, they did not bring up a site that was a good match for the searcher's desires. But is that Google's fault? Possibly, and as such, you know they will correct their error by reducing the chances of bringing up that site again.

Is it the searcher's fault? Possibly. It could be that they didn't properly define their search relative to what they truly wanted to find.

Once Google and the searcher are out of the way, that just leaves the website. Is it the website's fault that the visitor bounced right back to do another search? Odds are pretty good that this is where the real fault lies. When a visitor bounces, that site did not do what was necessary to keep the visitor, engage the visitor, and deliver what they were seeking.

So another way to look at the key sentence is this...

If someone clicks on **your website** *in the search results and 5 seconds later is back at Google doing another search,* **your site failed to deliver!**

Your brochure, if you have one, is a physical object that contains static information. From the moment it is printed until the moment the last one is handed out or thrown away, it does not change. It's a leave-behind, something someone can refer to quickly if they need to be reminded of something.

Far too many businesses treat their website much the same way. Yet a website is not physical in nature. And it can be amazingly dynamic.

Think about Google's website. Not only does it dynamically respond to every search, but it is even getting smart enough to modify its results based on the needs and habits of each individual searcher. Google changes the way their site works all the time in an effort to better perform for the searchers.

Of course your business is not Google. You are trying to reach consumers or other businesses as potential customers. But shouldn't you change your website to better serve your audience? For your best success it must be changed, not willy-nilly but in a smart way.

That's what this book is about, getting you focused on those smart things that will make a difference in your visitor experience and help you get higher conversions. Let's look critically at your website so that you can make changes that will better keep your visitors. Let's upgrade your website user experience so that Google knows that when someone gets there, it's exactly what they wanted to see.

When Google sends visitors to your site, and those visitors like what they see and stay there, then you are helping Google achieve their vision of search perfection. Do that, and you'll make Google happy. And when Google is happy with your site, it can rank at the top of the search results, generating the traffic that can convert to become the lifeblood of your business.

CHAPTER 1
HOW DID WE GET HERE?

The internet began its surge in popularity in the mid-1990s. That was in the era of dial-up internet connections with blazing speeds finally pushing up to 28.8 kbps. That means 28,800 bits per second. To put that in perspective, that's approximately two pages of this book transmitted in a single second. These days many people are online with download speeds more than 1,000 times faster. Even at very common speeds today, this entire book could be transmitted more than six times in a single second.

But I'm getting ahead of myself. The fastest modems were eventually able to get theoretical speeds of up to 56,000 bits per second. These were the 56K modems. And everyone was excited to have that technology in their homes. This allowed nearly everyone to get online, exchange emails, and view some of the early websites.

Those early websites typically came with only one of two key features. There were those that worked, and there were those that looked good. Getting both of those features in a single site was rare.

There was good reason for this phenomenon. Some web developers were coming out of the computer science realm. They were programmers. Creating websites was a very simple task compared to other programming, so they could make websites work quite well. They understood, and could easily take into consideration, that less data being transmitted would mean more responsiveness over a slow internet connection.

The other developers came from the graphic design field. Their focus was on the appearance of the websites. They generated some of the early concepts of what websites could look like, if only someone had a fast enough connection. These sites worked great within the local network of a business, but when moved to the public internet many of these sites were notorious for long waits. These designers did not consider modem speed as a factor.

As internet speeds increased, these two perspectives merged so that people came to expect websites to both work good and look good.

But then the businesses that had websites began to wonder if anyone was really paying attention. Were there real people, real prospects, visiting their website? This was the time when the bigger businesses started advertising their website addresses in the offline world. You started to see URLs in TV commercials and on billboards and even in yellow page advertising.

During this same time, some of the search engines began to appear. The earliest form were the directories, attempting to organize websites into categories and subcategories. And that led to free-form search which was a lot easier for people to use and find what they really wanted.

When these search engines gained popularity, businesses came to realize that it was not as necessary to advertise offline. Success in television advertising would require someone to get off their couch, move to their computer, log in to their internet access account, and navigate to the address that was shown on TV.

Instead, with the rise of search engines, they could start to attract the people who were already sitting at their computer, those who were already online looking for stuff. Suddenly, the traffic rush was on. Every business wanted more traffic, more traffic, more traffic, and dare I say, more traffic!

That continued until one day, when some bright executive somewhere said, "Hey, we're getting all these visitors to our site, but how does that help us?"

Yes, the light bulb went on. Traffic was not enough. Businesses wanted, and needed, that traffic to convert. In other words, they need visitors to take action once they get to the website. The visitors have to identify themselves as potential leads by giving up their email address, or by picking up the phone, or by requesting something that could be mailed or emailed.

It is not until the website generates a lead that there is any chance of generating revenue. So we have come to the age where a site needs both traffic and conversion. Of course that's what your website has always needed, but now you are aware that you need both. I assume you knew that before picking up this book. In fact you are probably reading now because you are aware that your site needs both traffic and conversion, but for some reason it is missing one or both of these critical pieces.

To get traffic, your website has to be visible. It has to be found by your prospects. And when those prospects visit your site, your site must inspire them to convert, to take action. Therefore, in the pages that follow we will look at issues that impact visibility, traffic, and conversion.

The Dark Side of Search

Since traffic from search engines has been a focus for a long time now, there have been many schemes people have cooked up to game the system. Basically they are looking at ways to influence the search results so they can get better visibility. They want to get around uniqueness, relevancy, and popularity by coercing the search engines to insert their website in a top spot. (If you're not familiar with my usage of the terms uniqueness, relevancy, and popularity go back and read the Introduction.)

The number of times a specific phrase exists on a web page can be a relevancy indicator. This realization led to a phenomenon called "keyword stuffing." There was a time when you could use a keyword phrase over and over again within a website and use that to convince a search engine that your site was relevant for that phrase. After all, the logic went, if your page uses the keyword 100 times, your page must be more relevant to that phrase than a site that uses the phrase only 5 times.

As an idea for relevancy, this makes sense, but the implementation did not. We ended up with websites that could be easily found, but they were often unreadable or just looked bad with many words repeated at the bottom. The search engines caught on and adjusted.

The number of links to a site can be a popularity indicator. The number and quality of such links still does play a role in this. But there was a time when quality did not matter and it was purely based on numbers. You have seen web pages with lots of links to unrelated websites. Typically the owners of those sites joined some kind of linking scheme where they would trade links with one another. "I'll link to your site if you link to mine." There are more sophisticated schemes too.

I bring up these examples, to point out that there are methods that should be avoided. There always have been, and, quite likely, there always will be tricks that someone discovers. Websites that try to get around the common sense factors of uniqueness, relevancy, and popularity will eventually fail. Those who implement these "black hat" techniques are the ones who fear the animals in the Google Zoo. Each algorithm update signals a change, and possible elimination, of their website from the search results.

The good news is that you do not have to engage in any such tactics. There are simple actions you can take to improve your website and the results you get. Tricks might work in the short-term, but they are risky. It's best to stick with what will always work.

How Did Your Website End Up Like This?

Over the past 20 years of website development I have seen two major pitfalls in the web design process. Both of these are extensions of the early days of website design. You will remember that I mentioned the two types of websites, those that <u>worked</u> and those that <u>looked good</u>.

Today, when contemplating a new website project for a business, many business people still think along those lines. Well, actually, they do not ask themselves if they want a website to work or if they want it to look good, they assume it can do both. But where the process breaks down is that they typically consider either the graphic design angle or the technical angle.

Many websites are treated similar to print projects. These are the websites coming from the graphic design side of web development. The mentality is that the website must be perfect before it is launched. Then, once the site is finally released for the world to see, it is never touched again. It was created to mimic a brochure. It's an online brochure. The only advantage of this site over a printed brochure is that the developers tend to include more information.

On the other hand, many websites are treated like I.T. projects. These are the ones developed by programmers or other technical people who are not as concerned about the appearance. Sometimes there are cool new features included in the site. They can include some cutting edge bells and whistles that other sites don't have. While there is great concern over website functionality, there is often very little focus on bottom-line business performance. One exception to this is that these high-tech sites may integrate well with various business systems such as accounting, CRM, inventory, and other databases.

There are problems with both of these website development styles. One significant problem shared by both is the mentality that expense must be minimized. These sites are viewed as necessary evils for doing business, so the goal is to produce a site that costs as little as possible. After all, they believe, "we need the site for credibility in case someone is looking." But they really do not expect much from their site. In this case their low expectations, and related development decisions, will lead to a self-fulfilling prophecy. Yes, they will have a website, but it will not do much of anything for their business.

What's the natural evolution of the two scenarios I have just described? As you read you might have already given a sigh of relief because your company considered both the design and the function. You might be letting yourself off the hook because you combined these angles from the beginning. Sorry to disappoint you, but I am not advocating a simple combination as the correct approach. Yes, you do need graphic design. Yes, you do need proper technical function. But your approach must not simply merge the two styles. Your approach must come from a different mind-set.

The Major Flaw in Websites

Let me explain this another way. The different approaches to website development, as well as the combined version, all lead to the same results, the same problem. I can best explain this with a new car analogy.

You know that while a brand new car is still on the dealer's lot, it is the best it will ever be. The moment you drive away, it loses value, it ages, it's on its way toward becoming obsolete. You know this is true because you have likely experienced it. But even if you have not, you've certainly heard the story over and over again.

Most people think about their website in much the same way. They pay a good deal of money to have a site developed, and they think that the day it is published is the best it will ever be, and that it will begin to become obsolete from that point on.

And so, you get a website and start the clock, counting down to the day that you will have to replace it. Then the countdown clock expires. It's time to get a new website. At this point you take one of three predictable responses.

1. You delay. The logic is that if it never produced, even when it was at its best, then why waste time or money on a new one? So inaction becomes the norm. After all, you don't need another expense.

2. You go to the other extreme, falling for a sales pitch that says you need to spend big bucks to get good results. This follows the "you get what you pay for" logic. Sometimes it's true, but not universally so.

3. You combine those two responses, into an ill-conceived hybrid. You spend big bucks, but then stall the publishing of your site, waiting until it's perfect. I've seen businesses stall the publishing of completed sites for more than a year because they wanted it to be "just right" the moment it launched. Again, they are thinking that the day it "goes live" is the best it will ever be.

Yet, here's the reality...

The day you publish your website is the <u>worst</u> it should ever be.

That's because everything you do before publishing is just a guess. It might be a good guess. It might be a guess based on research. It might be a guess based on what has worked for someone else. But in the end, it really is just a guess.

Need proof that it's a guess, consider this... How can your website developer possibly know what will cause <u>your audience</u> to take <u>your preferred action</u> at the highest possible level? They don't! And, they can't because your audience is unique and the action you want them to take is unique.

Remember, your web developers are most likely computer programmers or graphic designers. Sure, they are highly qualified developers, but think about this... Who knows the most about your business, about your prospects? You do. And do you know what causes your web-based audience to take your preferred action at the highest possible level? Probably not. And if you don't, how will anyone else?

Perhaps you think I'm wrong. Perhaps you think you do know the answer. But if you did, wouldn't you have communicated that to your web developers? Wouldn't your website already be performing at the level you need? The fact that you are reading this book tells me you are not getting the results you want, that your website is not performing good enough, not performing to your expectations.

The problem is that even if you know how to convert your prospects in a one-on-one sales meeting, that doesn't mean they'll respond the same way on your website. That knowledge might be a good starting place, but as far as your website is concerned it is only a guess, because you have not implemented your message successfully on this platform before.

But don't feel bad. To put this into perspective, think about the highest paid advertising professionals in the world, the marketing think-tanks, the Madison-Avenue types, who have been working on television ads for years. How often do they create advertising that fails? All the time. Consider all the Superbowl commercials that are amusing, but never appear again. Flops! If they worked wouldn't you continue to see those ads?

Sure, sometimes they get it right. And sometimes they get a super hit, but usually that's after a lot of testing and improving along the way.

And, so it's the same with your business website. You create it with certain goals in mind. Then you publish. And then the testing should begin. It should be worked, manipulated, changed, to get better results over time. It should continue to evolve, improve, never be allowed to get stagnant. And, as long as it keeps working, you would know that you do not need a new website. In fact, when your site is working, the only reason to replace it is to take advantage of new technology that could allow you to capture even more leads and/or sales.

You know what all this testing, measuring, and changing of your website is called? It's called marketing. The success of your website is all about marketing! From the day it is conceived, all the while it generates leads and sales, up until the day it is replaced, it's a marketing project. By thinking of your website as marketing, you can achieve market dominating results. Yes, you can still use your favorite graphic designers and your I.T. people, but do not lose site of the fact that **this website is your marketing project.**

CHAPTER 1 – KEY POINTS TO REMEMBER

Your website is your marketing project. You can use technology and graphic design to improve the site, but it should be controlled by marketing.

The day your website is published is the worst your website should ever be.

If your website continues to evolve, continues to get better and better, there's no need to pay for a new website. The only reason to replace a working website is to take advantage of new technology that may allow you to capture even more leads and/or sales.

CHAPTER 2
7 COMPONENTS OF AN EFFECTIVE WEBSITE

There are seven basic components required in an effective website. Each of the next seven chapters is dedicated to one of these components. While necessary, none of them will be as effective as you want unless you start out by researching the market that your business is in. Therefore, before I get to the seven components, I want you to begin with research.

The research is not technically part of your website, but it is part of your marketing. And since you are leading with marketing instead of design or technology, you are going to start with research. The results of the research will impact what goes into your site. The research will lead to better decisions and help you implement the seven components that your site needs.

For best results, do the research for your business and your website as you go through this short chapter. If you have completed similar research in the past, congratulations, you have a head start.

I also encourage you to take action right away in each of the following chapters. Once you start going through the seven components of an effective website, you will see improvements that should be made. If you have the ability to change your site yourself, do it. If you need to start a list so that you can hand it off to your web developer, do that. You ought to record all desired changes somewhere, or else you risk taking no action.

I assure you that reading this information and taking no action will provide no benefit to your bottom line.

In the Introduction I said that relevancy is, "the relationship between your site and the search words chosen." When we talk about the search words for your website they are most often referred to as "keywords" or "keyword phrases." In order to boost the relevancy of your site, you must consider the keyword phrases that your prospects will be using when they are looking at the Google search page. Consider your target market. Who are they? What is going on in their minds? What problems are they looking to solve? What are they going to search for?

It is important to know this information so that these words can be included within the context of your website. Several of the seven components of an effective website require your site to connect with your visitors on the level of the words chosen. So getting an understanding of what visitors are looking for is a good place to start your website improvement process.

In most cases, when a new website is built, there is some consideration for this, but not any significant research. Often the knowledge a business has about their own industry will skew their impression of the marketplace. For example, I recently did some research for the owner of a window treatments business. One of the areas of concern was over the industry phrase "custom draperies." Is that the right phrase to focus on?

Keyword Research

Google offers a free tool called the Keyword Planner. By using this tool you can see how many searches are performed on a global level, within a country, state, city, or any combination of the above. It's easy to research the behavior of searchers within your market.

The chart below shows actual data extracted from Google's Keyword Planner. It is a comparison of two search phrases, along with the number of searches for those phrases in an average month.

Search terms	Avg. monthly searches	Suggested bid
custom curtains	4,400	$2.48
custom draperies	1,300	$3.39

This real-life example is an excellent case study because there's often a difference between the phrases used by interested searchers and the phrases used within an industry.

My client pointed out that the proper phrase within the industry is "custom draperies," yet the data reveals that prospects are searching for "custom curtains" at a rate of nearly 3.5 to one. The number of times the phrase "custom draperies" is searched, using Google, during an average month, is 1,300 while the average for "custom curtains" is about 4,400 times.

The other interesting bit of information from this report is the suggested bid. This is for those who wish to advertise using Google and is based on the current competitive landscape. If you want your ad to show up, Google is suggesting you bid $3.39 for "custom draperies." The bid for "custom curtains" is much less, at $2.48. That tells us that advertisers are more concerned about "custom draperies" than "custom curtains" and have pushed the bidding higher for the former, even though there is a much smaller audience.

This demonstrates the importance of research. Advertisers that simply pursue the phrases that seem correct within their industry might be paying too much, and they might not be properly targeting their desired audience.

Of course, this report from Google is not the only tool you can use for market research. Furthermore, testing may reveal that users searching for "custom draperies" are closer to a buying decision than those searching for "custom curtains." I'm not saying that's true, but if research proves it is, then the former might warrant a higher bid price. But if testing does not reveal that condition, then lower advertising costs for a larger market would appear to be the better way to go.

A nice feature of the Google Keyword Planner is that it will make suggestions about related phrases. So even if you start with your industry-insider phrases, Google will present you with many additional phrases that are closely related to the terms you used. This way you can find other options to consider.

Keyword research is very important. Take a look at these resources. The Google Keyword Planner is available through Google Adwords by going to **adwords.google.com/KeywordPlanner**. If you do not already have a Google account you can get one for free. I have put together a short video to show you how to create your own account. I have also created a keyword research training video that shows you how to use the keyword planner. Both of these videos are available to you at **www.dominatethetop.com/bonus**.

Commercial Intent

Next, you ought to consider "commercial intent." That is, when the searcher is searching, are they looking to make some kind of transaction? Or are they simply gathering information? If their goal is to transact business, then there is commercial intent.

For example, if someone searches for "golf clubs" do you know why they are searching, what their intent is? Probably not. The phrase is too generic. They might be starting their research for a new set of clubs, but you cannot really tell. However, if the searcher looks for "callaway golf clubs" they are looking for information on a specific brand. That is a step closer to commercial intent. If they searched for "Callaway XR Pro Drivers" you can be reasonably certain they have commercial intent. That might not be the model they ultimately purchase, but to search for a specific model generally means the field is getting narrow, and they are looking for a provider. On the other hand, if someone searches for "how do I know which golf club to use" there is no commercial intent. They are just seeking an answer to their question.

Want to know a word that almost always indicates commercial intent? That word is "review." Interested buyers might search for "Callaway XR Pro Drivers review."

If someone searches for a product name, or even a business name, and then follows it with the word "review" then they are serious buyers. The reason is that when people are actively searching for reviews they have made a decision that this product or business is worth considering. Now they want to reach certainty and are looking for extra information to back them up on, or talk them out of, that decision.

If you want your website to attract the searchers who are most likely to do business with you, then bias your keywords toward commercial intent. Of course there might be some research-level phrases that can predispose searchers to your business so that they come back when they are ready to buy. Those are good too, especially if you have a way to capture their contact information and market to them later.

Keep these points in mind as you consider keyword phrases. Ask yourself if someone searching for this phrase is in a buying frame of mind. If the answer does not seem obvious to you, here's a sneaky way to find out. Let Google tell you!

Go to Google and search for the phrase you're considering. See what comes up near the top of the results. Are the websites that appear providing research type answers, or are they showing other vendors trying to sell in that industry? If the latter, it's more commercial intent.

For example, here's a search for "golf." The search results show general information, including a Wikipedia listing. Therefore Google does not view this as a search with commercial intent.

Compare that to a search for "Callaway XR Pro Drivers." Here the top listings and the right side are riddled with paid advertising. This search clearly represents one of commercial intent. Google believes that someone doing this search is ready to buy.

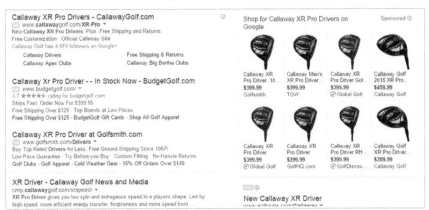

Remember, Google wants to deliver exactly what the user is searching for. That means they have to consider commercial intent. You can see it right in the search results.

Competition

Another part of your research is to take a look at the competition in your local market, especially if your primary audience is within a specific geographic region. In that case you can take your top search phrases, the ones with commercial intent, and do a search yourself to see what websites show up. Don't just look at the first page of the search results, but click through to the next page and the next until the sites that show up don't match your intended search very well. How many real, competing websites are there in your market? Then try another phrase. How many websites are there? This is important because if your site is not on the list and you are trying to get it there, this quick review shows the list of sites you will have to overcome.

At the top of the Google search results page, Google shows the total number of results. Do not be concerned about this number. Regardless of whether Google has 100,000 results or 100 million results, your competition does not extend that deep. Google doesn't even bother to show results past 1,000 even if someone wanted to look there. Therefore the top search results number is only an indicator as to the number of web pages that exist that might have some content related to the phrase or words within the phrase. Consider this number useless for your research! The number of real competitors in the search results is good information, while the number of search results pages is not.

Let me try to clarify the above for you with some pictures. For example, if you have determined that "leadership training seminars" is a good phrase for your business and you serve a local audience in Milwaukee, then you could search for "leadership training seminars milwaukee." Upon doing so you might see that there are 164,000 results:

But then you would look down the actual results to see how deep your competition really goes. Surely there are not 164,000 real competing options in Milwaukee. Already on the second page you will see this:

Firefighter/Fire Officer Development Seminars - Milwaukee, WI
community.fireengineering.com/forum/topic/show?id...
Sep 13, 2011 - 1 post - 1 author
Firefighter/Fire Officer Development **Seminars** - **Milwaukee**, WI Date: ... The curriculum is modeled after the **leadership training** programs

That doesn't compete with your seminars. And when you take a look at the third page of the results, you find nothing there that represents the type of leadership training you offer. With 10 results per page, that means there are 19 competing results, at most. You might be able to eliminate a few more by clicking through to the sites and digging in a bit deeper.

When you take the proper actions to position your site in the search results, all you have to do is overcome 10 of those 19 competitors, and your site will be on the first page of the results. Doesn't that sound a whole lot easier than trying to overcome 164,000 competing results? See, the problem isn't as bad as it might have seemed.

Once you have a good idea of the keyword phrases that are appropriate for your business, from the perspective of searchers, commercial intent, and your competition in your local market, you are ready to start putting those phrases into good use. Using the seven components of an effective site, as detailed in the upcoming chapters, you can jump ahead of your real competitors in the search results.

CHAPTER 2 – KEY POINTS TO REMEMBER

Always start with research to discover what the keyword phrases your prospects are actually searching for.

If you want your website to attract the searchers who are most likely to do business with you, then bias your keywords toward commercial intent.

Determine how real competitors show up in the search results for your keyword phrases. These are the only results your site has to overcome for top positioning.

Two extra resources are available to help you with your keyword research. There is a bonus video showing the research process. It's available to you at **www.dominatethetop.com/bonus**.

Plus, the workbook at **www.dominatethetop.com/workbook**, will help you track commercial intent and competition.

CHAPTER 3
COMPONENT #1 – SEO ELEMENTS

According to Wikipedia, *Search engine optimization (SEO) is the process of affecting the visibility of a website or a web page in a search engine's "natural" or un-paid ("organic") search results. In general, the earlier (or higher ranked on the search results page), and more frequently a site appears in the search results list, the more visitors it will receive from the search engine's users.*

The primary focus of your website is to connect with your visitors so that they take the action you want them to take. Before your site can accomplish this, it must be visible. Someone must see the link to your website. Only then can they click and start the relationship.

There are three elements of your site that directly connect to the visitor when they see them in the search results. These three things are your web page title, web page description, and URL.

(When someone talks about search engine optimization they often refer to the adjustment of these basic on-site SEO elements. Keep in mind that for best success, SEO is often necessary, but it is not always sufficient. It is a starting point and ought to be considered for every website. However, if you stop there you might miss your greatest opportunities.)

Take a look at the following screen shot from a search results page for leadership training. The first line shows the title defined on the web page itself, "Leadership Training and Development for Youth and Adults." The second line shows the URL, the address of the website, in this case "www.groupdynamic.us". The final two lines contain the description of the web page as defined within the web page itself.

When someone does a search, and your website shows up in the search results, these three elements are displayed. And, to help the searcher connect with your site, the words they searched for are displayed in bold to help capture their attention.

Leadership Training and Development for Youth and Adults
www.groupdynamic.us/ ▾
Group Dynamic provides high-quality **training** sessions and workshops to help businesses and youth organizations reach their potential.

That makes these three elements your first chance to influence the searcher to click through to your page. But more than that, these give the search engine a brief summary of what your site is about.

You might want prospects to visit your site for 50 different reasons, but you do not get that much space in the title or description to explain those 50 different things. You are forced to summarize, since the limits are about 60 characters in the title and 160 characters in the description. Therefore the search engine can assume that you are choosing the most important things to include in the title and description. They can assume that the words shown here include some of your most relevant keywords.

Let's take a look at each of these elements in greater detail.

The Page URL

There is nothing more relevant to your site than your URL. It's the first thing that any search engine knows about your website even before they look at the content of the site.

Most businesses will choose a URL that represents their business name. After all, we all want name recognition, right? The unfortunate downside of this desire is that we pick names that tell who we are, not what we do. Unless you already have a well-known business, people are not likely to be searching for your business by name. They will search for your business based on the keywords that come to their mind when they are trying to solve a particular problem. That means they are looking for what you do, or what you have to offer. If there's a match between the keywords used and your URL, you have an advantage.

Fortunately, for most of us with existing websites, the advantage of keywords within the URL is decreasing. And this makes sense. As Google and other search engines learn how to more accurately read the content on your page, they do not have to rely on the URL to contribute as much value. Some sources claim the URL no longer matters at all, but I disagree with that statement for a couple reasons.

First, if all, or part of, the URL matches the searched phrase, those words in the URL will show up in bold in the search results. So while using a domain that exactly matches the search query no longer guarantees top placement in the results, it still attracts attention when it does appear on the page.

Second, the URL still provides valuable information about the website to the search engines and the searchers. For example, if you need help with your internet marketing and you see two domains in the search results, **upatdawn.biz** and **24x7internetmarketing.com**, which one is more relevant to you? Clearly the second one. That means you're more likely to click.

For each separate website you get a single domain. That's the part of your website address that you had to pay for which gets included on every page, the www.yourbusiness.com part. But each page of your site gets its own URL which is your domain followed by /page-name. The opportunity here is to create page names that match the keyword phrase you are targeting on that page. For example, consider the business Chocolate University Online. If you know full URL, www.chocolateuniversityonline.com/chocolate-classes, would you be able to guess what this page is about without going there?

The Page Title

Once the search engines get past your URL, and start looking at your actual site, what do they see then? Usually it's the title of the page, followed by the description of the page, then the actual content of the page.

As I mentioned in the URL section, the opportunity is to create additional pages which include your relevant keyword phrase within the title of the page. Not only does this tell the search engines what this particular page is about, it's also your first chance to grab the attention of the searcher when your site shows in the search results. So consider this the first part of your free advertising, a small text-based ad. You control this content, and the goal of this content is to get the click. You need a title that will get attention while using the keyword phrase that is on the mind of the searcher.

By this point in time, many website developers know they need to add a title to each page of your site. And, if you have a content management system in place that helps you easily add pages to your own site, it most likely includes the ability to customize the title for each page as well.

There are two mistakes I often see relative to page titles. The first is that the title is the same on every page of the website. In that case, it's most often the name of the business. This does not help you! Each page of your site should be unique. And if a page is unique, then each should have a title that describes the main point of that page.

Having a unique title on each page will help the search engines better understand what your pages are about while also giving the searchers more information to consider clicking through to your site.

The second most common error is a title that contains too much information. Remember that the title is limited to about 60 characters. Go beyond that and the title will likely get cut off in the search results.

Sometimes, especially with a content management system, part of the title stays the same on every page, while part of the title is customized on a per-page basis. If that's the case on your site, keep in mind that the part that stays the same on each page cuts into your 60-character total. That gives you fewer characters to work with to get your keyword phrases included.

Another important factor about the title is that the position of your keyword phrase makes a difference. You can get better results if the important phrase is closer to the beginning of the title. If it makes sense to put it in as the first words, that is the best choice. Again, this can be messed up by content management systems that insist on putting the static portion of the title first.

If your business name has to be within the title of each page, put it at the end if you have a choice. That way your keyword phrase is featured first. The reason this is significant is that searchers are often looking for what you do, not who you are.

Remember that while your title is important for the search engines, it also helps you get clicks to your site. There are many ways to include keywords in a 60-character long space. However, do not sacrifice readability for humans just to create something Google might like better. In most cases, Google is not your customer.

While a title like this, "pizza delivery, pizza places, pizza near me, pizza deals" surely represents some useful keyword phrases for a pizza restaurant that delivers, a better title might be, "Try Pizza Delivery from Joe's Pizza Emporium." That focuses on the "pizza delivery" keyword phrase while also giving the searcher additional information. Plus this title includes a verb, an action that the visitor can take.

Since the title is your first chance to influence the searcher, make it worthwhile. The title ought to give the searcher some insight into the page while reinforcing why that page is relevant to their search. The title you choose can be the most important piece of information to start the relationship with the searcher, to get their click!

Do you want to see what the titles of your pages are today? There are a couple of ways to do this. First, simply bring up your website in your browser. If you have a recent browser version, there will be tabs near the top of the browser. Each tab will display a single web page. The title shows up in the tab. (For older browsers, the title shows up in the bar at the top of the window.) If you cannot read the entire title because the tab is not long enough, move your mouse to hover over the tab. The entire title will be displayed.

The second method is a bit more difficult, but this method will reveal additional information including the description that I discuss in the next section.

Bring up your website in your browser. Right-click with your mouse on any empty part of the page. A small menu should appear. Choose "view source" or "view page source" from that menu. You will see all of the code that makes your web page look the way it looks. While you are looking at the source, click CTRL-F on your keyboard to open up a "find" box. Type in **<title>**. You should see a line that starts with **<title>** and ends with **</title>**. The characters in between represent the actual title of the page.

```
<meta http-equiv="Content-Type" content="text/html; charset=UTF-8" />
<title>Refugee Resettlement Support</title>
```

How does your title look? Is it too long, or missing completely? And, just as importantly, does it contain a good keyword for your business? If a searcher found this title in the search results, would it inspire them to click? If necessary, change your titles. If you do not have the ability to change titles on your own, make notes so that you can present a list of updates to your web developer. They ought to be able to easily make this change.

The Page Description (Meta Description)

The last of the three elements that show up in search results is the page description, often called the meta description. This description contains one or two sentences, approximately 160 characters maximum, in which you connect with the searcher and entice them to click. Ultimately you want to have a title and description pairing that is more captivating than those of the search results around yours. You want your listing to stand out in the crowd.

I already pointed out that each page of your site will have a unique title. For the same reasons, it also makes sense to have a unique description on each page. The description can reinforce the keyword phrase that you are targeting for that page. Once again, this helps tell the story to the search engine and helps with relevancy, but it is also very important for searchers.

When you are creating the title and description for any page, keep in mind these three things which will help your site get more clicks than those sites that are not as deliberate in their attempts:

- have your title grab the searchers' attention
- have your description relate to the searchers and identify with the problem they have
- offer a solution, or promise of a solution, if they click

Strangely, it seems that many website developers are not aware of the need for a description on each page. I see many websites where there is no description at all or where there is a description line in the code but it is empty. Those with the empty description are likely content-managed sites where no one has entered any descriptive text.

Besides complete absence of the description, two other common errors parallel the mistakes with the title. The first is using the same description on every page. And the second is writing a description that is far too long.

With descriptions there is a third problem that shows up quite frequently. That is a description that is too short. This is free advertising space. Use all of it. If you don't know what to say about the keyword phrase itself, you can add to it using an additional keyword phrase that is closely related to the primary phrase, or include some text that asks the searcher to take an action to visit your site. There are many ways to use up 160 characters. Try to get as close as you can without going over.

Unlike the title, you will not see your page descriptions in your web browser simply by visiting the site. Instead, you have to look at the code behind the scenes to see what the description looks like. The way you do this is just like the second method of looking at your title. Bring up your website in your browser. Right-click with your mouse on some empty part of the page. You should see a small menu appear. Choose "view source" or "view page source" from that menu.

You will see the HTML code that tells your browser how to display the page. While you are looking at the code, click CTRL-F on your keyboard to open up a "find" box. Type in **description**. You should see a line that starts with **<meta**, includes the text **name="description"**, and ends with **>**. Often the name="description" text immediately follows **<meta** as in the example below. Sometimes it appears right before the closing greater-than sign. In this line the actual description is the text in quotes after **content=**.

```
<meta name="description"  content="Website dedicated to the people
involved in refugee resettlement volunteer activities. Help 10 million
refugees find home! Tips, hints, and support here." />
```

If you see a line that contains **description**, but the format is different than this, then continue looking. You want to find the version that resembles this example. If you see nothing that looks like this, then you do not have a description on the page. It is time to remedy that situation.

Assuming you found a description, how does it look? Is it too long, or too short? And, just as importantly, does it contain a good keyword phrase for your business? If a searcher found this description in the search results, would it help them decide to click? As with the title, if you do not have the ability to change this on your own, make notes so that you can present a list of updates to your web developer.

(Note that Google does not promise to use your description in the search results. In some cases they will display different text. In their own words, "Google will sometimes use the meta description of a page in search results snippets, if we think it gives users a more accurate description than would be possible purely from the on-page content." Translation... make your description concise and accurate. That makes Google's job easier, and you get to present your own message to the searcher.)

Google offers a free tool called Webmaster Tools which will identify problems that exist within your page titles and descriptions. The tool points out duplicate meta descriptions, long meta descriptions, and short meta descriptions. The tool also shows if you have missing title tags, duplicate title tags, long title tags, short title tags, and non-informative title tags. It is very helpful to have this information given to you without having to look at each page on your own. You can get started with Google Webmaster Tools by creating an account at **www.google.com/webmasters/tools**. In Chapter 14 there is more information about using Webmaster Tools to find these problems.

Meta Keywords

Meta keywords are no longer part of basic SEO. I am bringing this up here because they are often used in the same sentence with the meta description as in, "We have to update the description and keywords on our site." The reason for this is that meta keywords can reside in the website's code right next to the meta description.

In the past, when search engines were trying to figure out what a web page was about simply by using the elements found in a page, the keyword tag was important. Unfortunately, being hidden in the code and unlimited in length, it quickly and easily became abused by people trying to rank their sites higher, even with phrases that did not apply to the content of the site. You can imagine how that did not please searchers who ended up on a site that had no chance of fulfilling their search request. As such, Google stopped using the meta keyword tag several years ago.

Other search engines may still give some measure of validity to the keyword tag. In that light, if you choose to use it, keep it highly focused. These days it is often better to have no keyword tag than to have a poorly constructed one. The most common problem I see with keyword tags is that they are often overstuffed. Limit them to the primary keyword phrase you are targeting for the page and perhaps a few very closely related phrases. A good rule of thumb is that the words in your meta keyword tag should also appear within the readable body text of the page itself.

To view the content of your keyword tag, you have to look at the source HTML again, just like you did to see the description. While you are looking at the code search for **keywords**. You should see a line that starts with **<meta**, includes the text **name="keywords"**, and ends with **>**. In this line the actual keyword list is the text in quotes after **content=**. If you have more than one keyword phrase, they should all be separated by commas.

```
<meta name="keywords" content="chocolate class, chocolate
classes, online chocolate classes, chocolate classes online">
```

Since you are updating titles and descriptions on your site anyway, is it time to make some change to the keywords list? You have two choices. Either trim the keyword list down to a few excellent keywords per page or remove the keywords meta tag completely.

Please Note

Titles, Descriptions, and Keywords are not the only SEO elements worth considering. But it is surprising how many times these are poorly implemented on business websites. If all you do is fix these three things, you will gain a search engine advantage over most of your competitors.

If you would like to get a little more advanced, I have pulled some additional SEO topics together into an external appendix. As a reader of this book, they are available for you to download at **www.dominatethetop.com/bonus**.

CHAPTER 3 – KEY POINTS TO REMEMBER

The goal of appearing in the search results is to get the click.

Your first chance to influence a searcher is based on the way your site appears in the results listing. You can control the title and description of your site as well as the URL.

Make sure the title gets attention while using the keyword phrase that is on the mind of the searcher.

Create a description that connects with searchers and entices them to click.

CHAPTER 4
COMPONENT #2 – TEXT QUANTITY & QUALITY

The Google algorithms are learning to read and understand what they read. That means that both the quantity and quality of text on a web page is important for SEO. Of course the text on the page is also important for the human experience. Ultimately your website must serve your human visitors. That means HEO, Human Experience Optimization, is critically important.

This is a good place to point out that the human experience must be your top priority. There are many ways to get visitors to your website that have nothing to do with SEO. Therefore sacrificing any human experience element simply to get a potential boost in the search results does not make sense. And as Google algorithms get smarter, they will be looking to emulate the human experience.

When discussing the text on a page, quantity is the easier of the two to discuss. In Google's own words, "Create a useful, information-rich site, and write pages that clearly and accurately describe your content... Try to use text instead of images to display important names, content, or links. The Google crawler doesn't recognize text contained in images."

Google refers to quantity as a factor in being "information rich." Imagine a web page with 10 words of text and another page with 300 words of text. Which one can best explain what the page is about? In the vast majority of cases, 300 words stands a better chance of conveying the right idea. 300 words allows for a much greater level of information richness than 10 words.

Of course you have to balance this with the graphical elements on your site. A text-only website might be great for Google to understand, but it could be quite dull for your human visitors. If a picture is worth a thousand words, then include the picture, and also explain the message the picture is meant to convey. After all, humans have different learning styles too. Some of your site visitors will love the images and understand them immediately, while others will prefer to read the words.

Regarding the quality of the text on a page, we have to strive for a balance between traffic and conversion. Therefore, to have quality text means we are appealing to the search engines to boost their understanding of our site, while simultaneously appealing to the visitors to boost their conversion rate. We want them to take action once they get to the site.

From the perspective of search engine quality, Google says,

"Think about the words users would type to find your pages, and make sure that your site actually includes those words within it."

In the research phase, you determined the most important keyword phrases. In the previous chapter of this book we looked at having individual pages of your site targeted to specific keywords. Then we included those phrases in the title and description. Now you must work your keyword phrases into the body text. In some cases it's OK to simply include phrases as bullet items, but you'll get the best results, and be more relevant to the searcher, if you work your most important keyword phrases into the context of the page.

There are those who suggest that keyword phrases should be included within specific elements of the page. For example, there are different heading levels (referred to as h1, h2, ... h6) within the HTML programming of a web page. There is regular paragraph text, bullets, bold text, italicized text, and underlined text. And there are other spots where text can be placed. The "rules" for keyword placement in these areas can change. In general it seems to be a good thing to include the most important keyword phrase within a heading or emphasized within a paragraph. But the most important thing of all is to use the keyword in a natural sense.

Remember, I said that Google is learning to read and understand. This is leading to the concept of "over-optimization." Some businesses have tried so hard to optimize their websites for search engines that they have created poor quality for their real users. A few years back this might have worked. I have previously seen recommendations to include the target keyword phrase within every possible part of the page. Years ago I even did this in some cases. But unless you want to fear every new Google algorithm change that comes along, there's no reason to play games. As Google understands your site better with each update, the sites that best explain their position relative to their keyword phrase will win out in the quality battle.

You ought to strive for human readability. Yes, include the keyword phrase and related phrases as they make sense. But these days "keyword stuffing" is going to get your site penalized. If you're not sure what I mean, here's an example of a paragraph stuffed with the phrase "solar panels." I'm sure you have encountered a website with text like this...

"High quality solar panels can be quite harsh on the pocketbook. Before purchasing solar panels, you must know exactly what type of solar panels you need as well as the payment terms offered for those solar panels.

> *"It's also important for you to know beforehand that solar panels installation is rather permanent. Solar panels will stay in place for many years to come. And when you move out, you will leave your solar panels behind."*

That is junk. No one would talk like that. It's not natural. It's written only for the search engines, not for the human visitors. Stay away from this type of wording.

So how does all this translate into the placement of keyword phrases on a page? Typically using a phrase once or twice is often enough, as long as there are alternate ways of saying the same thing. If it makes sense to do so, include some keywords in bold, italic, or underline. But be certain that this is beneficial to your human visitors. Also, including a heading or subheading on the page is often a good idea because it breaks up the page, making it easy for someone to skim your content. If the keyword phrase in that position adds value to the content, then it's win-win. It benefits the reader and gives Google something to work with.

Here are a few suggestions to help you judge the quality of the text on your page.

Three Quality Tests

The first test is the **Conversation Test**. Read your page out loud, as if it's part of a spoken conversation. When you come to any heading or subheading, say "Wait, I need to tell you about..." followed by the heading. Then continue speaking the next paragraph. If it all flows naturally, similar to the way you would talk, and it sounds good, then the text is likely in good shape.

The second test is the **Semantic Test**. Grab the text from your page, remove the keyword phrase completely, and see if you can still tell what the page is about. If you can, then you have created enough supporting meaning through other word usage. Your overall keyword placement is probably about right.

There is another factor related to the quality of the text on the page. That is, who is it written for? We can call this the **Audience Test**. Is the text on the page all about your business or is it all about the visitors? You do care about your site visitors, don't you? You want them to convert, to take the action you want them to take. Therefore you must appeal to them. You must care about them and their experience on your site.

One simple way to accomplish this is to...

Talk more about your visitors than you do about your own business.

I know what you're thinking, "doesn't a visitor come to my website to learn about my business?" Sure, that might be true, but that's not the primary reason. First and foremost, visitors arrive at your website because they are trying to solve their problem. This does not mean that you must ignore your own business. There is a time and place for tooting your own horn. It's just not right now, when a visitor arrives at your site. You will see better options later in this book.

For now, consider your website as if it is part of the conversation you are having with a visitor. If you're at a party, or even a business networking event, and you meet someone who dominates the conversation, talking relentlessly about him or herself, you would get tired of it and want to get away. The same feelings come up when a person visits a website that talks about itself without regard for the visitors. Visitors will leave. It's so much easier to get away from an annoying website than an annoying person. At the first sign of trouble, any visitor can click the back-button and do another search.

To avoid becoming discarded in favor of a different website, you have to shift your focus to your potential customer. Write the content of each page in terms of "you" more often than terms of "we," "us," and your company name. This is pretty easy to verify. Look at your page and count the instances of each. Then, if necessary, rewrite the copy so that you are addressing your visitor. If you would like a quick and easy tool to analyze any web page and give you the findings, try **www.CustomerFocusCalculator.com**.

Now that you have begun to think about your website visitors, you are ready to embrace HEO and address the remaining components of an effective website.

CHAPTER 4 – KEY POINTS TO REMEMBER

Work your best keyword phrases into the text within the appropriate pages of your site.

Have at least 300 words of text on any page that you wish to rank well in the search engines. (400 or more words is even better.)

Judge the quality of web page text by using the three quality tests:
- The Conversation Test
- The Semantic Test
- The Audience Test

Check your site at **www.CustomerFocusCalculator.com**.

CHAPTER 5
COMPONENT #3 – ANSWER THE 3 QUESTIONS

Let's say you have done a great job with keyword research. Relative to your keyword phrases, you are doing fantastic with uniqueness and relevancy. Your site has started to appear often enough in the search results. You have crafted a great title and a compelling description. A searcher notices your listing among the various choices. They take the next step and decide to click. They end up on your website. Perfect!

Now what do you want them to do? You want them to take some kind of action: to call you, to buy something, to sign up on your email list, whatever.

But before they can do any of those things, they have to decide to stay on your website. The back button is so easy, the relationship so tenuous. Clearly the odds are stacked against you. When someone first arrives on a web page they haven't seen before, their initial impression is made subconsciously in less than 1 second.

Within a handful of seconds they have already decided whether they like, or don't like, the site. And within 10-20 seconds they have decided the site is worth looking at, or not, and they are taking action accordingly.

From the perspective of your visiting audience, you must make sure the page addresses the reason they clicked through in the first place. So, what can you do to hold onto your visitors, to get them to stay on your site when their overriding thought is "what's in it for me?" To address this, and keep them around long enough, you have to answer three questions that are running around in between their ears...

1. Where am I?
2. What offer can I take advantage of?
3. Why should I choose you?

Let's take a quick look at each of these.

The first question they are asking is, "where am I?" The searcher just clicked and went somewhere new. They have not seen your site before, and they don't know what they will find, though they have expectations which they hope are met. They are searching for something and decided that your site offered the potential to fulfill their needs. But now, as your site fills their browser window, they are momentarily disoriented. Can you relieve them of this disorientation? Can they quickly determine that your site provides a solution to their problem?

The second question, "what offer can I take advantage of" gets to the heart of "what's in it for me?" They came to your site for a specific reason, and you helped them overcome their initial disorientation. This caused them to stay around long enough to see that your business has the potential to overcome their problem. Now they want to find what you specifically have to offer.

What advice, knowledge, product, or service does your site offer that they can evaluate further? An offer can be something as simple as a link to another page that has more details about a service that might fulfill their needs. Or an offer could be information about a specific product that solves their problem. An offer, in this sense, is something that helps move visitors forward toward their desired goal. And, after their disorientation is relieved, something on that page has to grab their attention. Do they sense any promise in staying longer? What benefit will they receive if they delay a return to search?

Finally, if your site makes it past the visitor's first two questions, they quickly arrive at the third and ask, "why should I choose you?" In other words, they are asking what evidence do you have that gets them comfortable enough to consider further engagement with your business?

Their internal credibility sensor is on high alert. Two potential outcomes from this internal sensor are boredom and disbelief. These are opposite ends of the spectrum, and yet ride very close together. There's not much room in between. If your site is rather dull, creating no excitement, then, yawn, there's no compelling reason for visitors to act. On the other hand, if you attempt to create too much excitement, it can be interpreted as hype, and the site loses believability.

I would like to spend a little more time on the subject of the third question, "why choose you?" because this is where many businesses try to add some excitement and often, unintentionally, do the opposite.

Several years ago, I hosted a website training series called the "Web Genius Summit." During these sessions I had the pleasure of interviewing Ann Convery. Ann is an international speaker, seminar leader, trainer, and author who has worked with top professionals across a variety of industries. Our topic of conversation was how to attract more clients in 30 seconds or less. This can be applied to an "elevator speech," but my interest was in applying this knowledge to websites.

Our conversation revolved primarily on the function of the primitive part of our brains. That's the part that is completely self-centered, likes contrast, and is triggered only by emotion. Yet this is the part of the brain that makes the final decision. Any conversation, whether in person, or as text on your website, must appeal to these primitive characteristics.

To demonstrate how this works in the human mind, consider a recent tragedy that you heard about in the news. It might have been weather-related, or a shooting, or a serious car accident. Typically when you hear this news your first thought, one that happens instantly, is quick relief that you were not there. Then you might do a mental calculation about others you know personally, hoping they were also not there. And, then, finally, you think about the seriousness and how sad it is for those who were there as well as their friends and family. That's our primitive brain working.

When your website addresses the "what's in it for me"-related questions, it's appealing to the self-centeredness of the primitive brain. One of the other characteristics of the primitive brain is that it only responds to easy-to-understand concepts. From a psychology standpoint, these would be things low on Maslow's hierarchy of needs such as safety, security, love, and health. Whenever you can appeal to your audience at this level, your chance of keeping the visitors engaged on your site goes way up. If you start using advanced concepts then you are asking your visitors to think too much.

The problem that Ann pointed out to me is that in business we often use what she calls "unhearable" words. These are neutral, yet abstract phrases, and phrases that are exhausted, overused. Some examples may include statements like, "we can help take your business **to the next level**," "our team thinks **out of the box**," "you will enjoy our **integrated approach**," "we've got the **next generation**," "you'll get **the life of your dreams**." You get the idea. Seriously, what do any of these phrases really mean? You don't know what they refer to unless you carefully consider them in the context of your life or other material.

Phrases like these on your site will cause visitors to flee.

As visitors are subconsciously deciding whether or not to stay on your site, these types of messages simply do not grab them the way you intend. Best case scenario they stop forward progress. Worse, they might trigger the yawn. And the phrase "the life of your dreams," if you successfully do get someone to pause and think about it, likely raises disbelieve. "Yeah, sure. My dreams are pretty big. I doubt you can get me there." Click. Gone.

Instead, stick to concepts that are not abstract and do not require thought. In other words, focus your message on what is in it for your site visitors. These are often the benefits of what your business offers. Connect these benefits to a basic emotion such as love, health, money, or time and you will stand a better chance of connecting with your visitors because almost everyone wants more of these things. If you demonstrate that you can connect their needs to your solution, and you have an offer they can take advantage of without thinking, then you have done well.

So consider these questions: where am I, what offer can I take advantage of, and why should I choose you? Answer them well, and you have earned a visitor that might stick around long enough for you to engage with them.

Here's a simplified example. Imagine that you want to find some information online. You want a website that can help you do a search. Assume for a moment that you are not familiar with Google and Yahoo. A friend gives you the URLs to put into your browser. You end up here:

Or here:

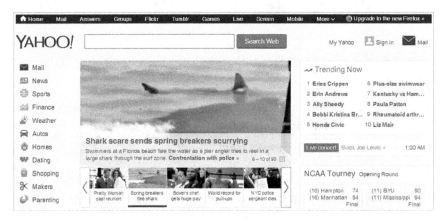

If you were told where you were going with each URL, to a site called Google and a site called Yahoo, respectively, when you typed the URLs into your browser, which of these sites would relieve disorientation faster? To answer the first question, "where am I," you will know that you are on the correct site with each of them, but Google has less clutter so your disorientation diminish quicker there.

The second question relates to the offer. You want to search, so which one allows you to do this best? Well, they both do, but which one makes it obvious without any further thought? Google does. The Yahoo site is quite distracting if all you want to do is search.

For the third question, "why choose you," consider love, health, money, and time. Is a search engine going to help you with any of these directly? In this case I would say the direct impact is on time. Google wins this too because you will waste no time from the moment you arrive until the first search results come up. Maybe these three factors contribute to why Google has about two-thirds of the search engine market share and Yahoo has about 10%. People choose Google.

CHAPTER 5 – KEY POINTS TO REMEMBER

In order for your website to keep visitors around long enough to engage with your business, your site must answer their three initial questions:

1. Where am I?
2. What offer can I take advantage of?
3. Why should I choose you?

Your website must appeal to the primitive brain that enjoys easy-to-understand concepts without having to engage in thought.

If you haven't done so already, go to the workbook and follow the prompts for the three questions. This will help you improve your visitor experience.

If you don't have the workbook, you can download your own copy at **www.dominatethetop.com/workbook**.

CHAPTER 6
COMPONENT #4 – DEFINE PAGE GOALS

Congratulations, your site visitor stayed beyond those initial crucial seconds. You have an opportunity to establish a relationship with him. Now what? What do you want the visitor to do next?

To be effective in any marketing campaign, you need goals. What are you trying to achieve with this website anyway? This big-picture goal is a good starting point because it's likely that you have already considered it. Of course if your goal was "we need a website" and now you have one, it's no wonder it doesn't perform. In this case your goal of getting a website has already been met. If your goal envisioned a future beyond the creation of your website, then what is that ultimate goal? And how does that apply to your site's visitors?

Do you want your site visitors to think more highly of your business before they leave? If you built a site to give your business credibility, that might be all that happens. Or is your goal for the visitors to pick up the phone and call, or to provide you with their email address? If so, then the goal for your website is lead generation.

Perhaps the goal is to have your website complete a sale. That would be the case if your desire is to conduct ecommerce. Maybe the goal is to educate the consumer or get donations. There are many different types of goals you can have with a website. Your job is to know what that goal is. And, is that goal compatible with the goal that your site visitor is trying to achieve? **Does your goal solve their problem?**

For simplicity moving forward, I will sometimes refer to your ultimate goal as a sale even though it may differ in your business. Just keep in mind that when I say "sale," I mean the goal you are trying to achieve, whatever it is.

But this generalized, overarching goal is not really what I'm asking you to consider at this point. Your high level goal is a prerequisite. You have to have that figured out before you can consider this fourth element in making your website effective. What I want you to consider now are the "micro conversions." In other words, what is the goal of the single page that the visitor is on?

Every page should attempt to move someone into or through your sales funnel toward the ultimate desired action. How does an individual page in your site do that? And, for best results, how does it do that without making your visitor stop to think about it?

Don't worry if this is difficult or if you think you might get this wrong. We all get it wrong all the time. The nature of marketing is often to...

Take your best guess based on what you know.

Just don't deceive yourself into thinking that you know the absolute right answer. If you believe you have the right answer then there is no room for improvement. Since we always want improvement, we have to believe that our initial guess simply serves as a stake in the ground, a starting place. Always assume there are ways to improve upon the initial guess.

In fact, the problem with most websites, the reason many never get the response they could get, is that they were built with the first guess that came along and often without a clear marketing purpose.

Then the site was never changed, thus staying with that initial guess even after it proved to be a poor guess.

The reality is that no matter how well you know your business and your customers, and no matter how good your website developer is, your website project began with a guess. Once again, I can say this with some confidence here, because if that guess had been wildly successful, you probably would not be reading this book.

Later on I will show you a way to test your site to improve upon your guess and get better results. For now, accept that your best guess is appropriate and useful.

OK, let's say your site has successfully kept a visitor, and she is on a specific page. It might be the home page of your site, but it might not be. Depending on her search, the page she clicked on might have put her somewhere deeper in your site. Therefore you must consider each page independently. Some pages may truly fit the ultimate goal for your site. These are the pages designed to capture the sale, set up the phone call, or induce the action of whatever your ultimate conversion goal is.

You cannot reach for the sale on every page of your site without turning people off. Imagine you're at a party talking to someone and with every subject change they try to offer you products or services that you might be interested in. "Oh, you like to ski? You should check out the new XYZ boots that you can get for $X," "Next time you order pizza go to ABC Italian Restaurant," "I represent this great line of weight loss products." Yikes! If this were the first time you met that person, you would never want to have another conversation.

Consider that this may be the first time someone has ever landed on your website. True, the people who visit are looking for something. At this point it seems there's the potential for your business to provide a solution. How do you satisfy their needs and get them to the point of also satisfying yours?

Micro Conversions

The key is in a term I threw out a little while ago... "micro conversions." This can be defined as a little step that someone takes in the right direction. Unless you have an ecommerce site, you might only have a single page in your website that makes the big push to your sale. What does every other page do to help get someone to that sales page? They have little enticements. "do this," "consider that," "more info," "click here."

Depending on where the visitor is in the sales process the next step might lead them to the sales page, but it might not. It might have to give them more information before that step would make sense to them.

Ideally you must consider the goal of each page within your site. But you don't have to do it all at once. If you think the idea of creating micro-conversions is too overwhelming, you won't take any action. So don't start thinking about your entire site right now. Just begin with your home page. Since this is the most likely starting point for your visitors, it is the most important one to improve. Once the goal is clear, then add the appropriate links, images, and whatever else is needed on the page to make that path obvious to the visitors.

Don't make them think about it. They should see the yellow-brick road and be eager to follow.

Once you have determined the goal for a page then ask yourself the question, "how might we accomplish this goal on this page?"

You cannot ask this question until you have a goal. And after you ask this question, a variety of answers may come to mind. Speed up the results by asking this question out loud to a small group of people. Do some brainstorming around it. Our brains love to answer good questions, so record all the ideas that come up.

Assuming you have several ideas to choose from, which do you try first? Remember that it is OK to guess. Make your best guess or see if you can get group consensus. Which idea seems as though it could give the best results? Then put the idea to the test. That is, implement it! Don't just sit on the idea, put it into practice right away.

Next, watch the results to see if you have influenced visitor behavior. You can look at your website's analytics[1] to see what changes happened relative to site usage behavior. Often a before-and-after snapshot will give a good impression as to whether the change made a significant impact. For more subtle measurements and to eliminate other factors, such as timing or seasonal buying patterns, a tool called the A/B Split Test can be very powerful. This topic is reserved for later. You'll find more in Chapter 11.

Often the steps needed for the micro-conversions are simply the inclusion of appropriate links to get the user to a page that best represents the next step in your sales funnel. These links have a couple of additional benefits beyond user behavior. One of the goals of this book is to help you put your website in a position to make Google happy. These internal links help Google better understand the content of your pages and the relationships between them. This helps them determine if some of your inner pages are most relevant to the user's search.

> **If you don't guide the visitors to the actions you want them to take, you are not getting the results you want.**

---

1 There are many different ways to look at your website analytics. Google Analytics is a free tool that requires you to add a little extra code to the pages of your website. Adding this code gives you access to a lot of additional helpful information. Your web host may also have some analytics available for you, free or for an extra charge. There is no Google Analytics data available until after you install the code. On the other hand, your web host is likely to have data on their server already. Ask them how you can get access to it.

Consider the importance of this. Each person who visits your site has their own motivations, their own reasons for clicking through to your site. They may be in different parts of their own buying cycle. If someone is much closer to the sale, do you want them starting at the beginning of your sales funnel? It might make sense for them to skip the first part, positioning them closer to the action you ultimately want for them. This internal linking helps Google deliver the visitor to the most relevant page on your site for their needs. And because the most relevant page may not be your home page, this reinforces why it is so important for you to consider the goals for each page separately.

As an example, consider the search for golf clubs that I mentioned back in the Commercial Intent section of Chapter 2. If you have a sporting goods business, and someone searches Google for "Callaway XR Pro Drivers" it wouldn't make any sense to have them land on your home page or even on the main golf clubs page. Clearly they know what they are looking for so there is no need to guide them through a longer funnel. If Google already understands the structure of your site, they can send the visitor directly to the specific page that best serves their need. Whereas if they came in with a vague idea of buying new clubs, they could enter at your golf clubs page where you might have some links to other pages that help them narrow down their own preferences and buying criteria.

After you have completed the modifications to your home page, then move on to the other major pages of your site. By major, I mean that they are one click from your home page. Many, if not all, of these pages are part of your website's navigation menu. So start there. If there are other links on your home page, outside of your main navigation, that can take someone to another page of your site, then consider those pages as well.

Finally, you can prioritize all the other pages on your site and take them in order. How can you set that priority? Following your gut feeling is a good place to start. What pages do you think are important? Which ones can best help guide your visitors to the action you most want them to take? What path will they follow to the ultimate sale?

Another option for prioritization, clearly more scientific in nature, would be to take a look at your website's analytics. Which pages are your most frequent landing pages? In other words, which pages are the most frequent entry points into your site?

In the example from Google Analytics that follows, over the past month the home page of the Chocolate University Online website was the entry point only 15.39% of the time. We should look down the list and make sure each of the top landing pages is ready to serve the visitor and the business goals.

Landing Page ?	Sessions ? ↓
	1,962 % of Total: 100.00% (1,962)
1. / home page	**302** (15.39%)
2. /chocolate-information/	**168** (8.56%)
3. /lp/chocolate-classes/	**145** (7.39%)

Besides landing pages, also look at the overall numbers as to which pages get the most visits regardless of the path to get there.

In the example shown on the next page, the same three website pages are the most visited. The numbers are higher in that chart than the one above. That means that these pages are not only entry points, but are also pages that people eventually visit even when they started on a different page. Specifically, if 302 visitors landed on the home page as their starting point (as shown above), but there were 390 page views (as follows), then the home page was viewed 88 times by visitors who did not start there.

Page ?		Pageviews ↓ ?
		2,913 % of Total: 100.00% (2,913)
1. /	⊡	**390** (13.39%)
2. /chocolate-information/	⊡	**252** (8.65%)
3. /lp/chocolate-classes/	⊡	**155** (5.32%)

For fastest impact, prioritize your updates with both of these high-visit categories; landing page and total pageviews. Your most visited landing pages will have maximum influence at the beginning of the relationship. Your pages with the largest overall numbers will touch the greatest number of visitors at some point. That makes this focus a good place to start.

The most important thing to consider, when you are thinking about your page goals, is to always keep your site visitors in mind. They are the ones you are trying to influence. The flow and the micro-conversions they follow must make sense to them. Each time they arrive on a new page, they will again ask themselves where am I, what offer can I take advantage of, and why should I choose you? The good news is that if they have traveled down your path, and then discover they're in the wrong place, they might just take a single step back. That's still in your site, not back to Google!

CHAPTER 6 – KEY POINTS TO REMEMBER

Is the ultimate goal of your website compatible with the goal of your site visitors?

Besides the overall website goal, consider the goal for each page of your site. Each can create a micro-conversion to move visitors toward your ultimate goal.

To systematically improve your website, start with changes to the top landing pages and the pages that are most visited. Then move to other pages within your site.

Use the workbook to list and track your page goals. If you don't have the workbook yet, go ahead and download your own copy at **www.dominatethetop.com/workbook**.

CHAPTER 7
COMPONENT #5: AIDA – FROM ATTENTION TO ACTION

You know a bad website when you see one. You do a search and click on a result that looks promising. Then, ugh, what is this!? You found a site that might have gotten the basic SEO correct and possibly has some good text, but the designers dropped the ball when it comes to answering your questions and guiding you along a goal path. But the big problem might be that there is nothing on the page to grab your attention, or perhaps there's too much vying for your attention. It's a mess of text and/or images and you don't know where to begin.

Your website serves a marketing function for your business. It is simply one of your available marketing tools. As such, all of the lessons of direct response marketing developed over the past century apply here. I will not even attempt to cover the vast amount of material available on this subject. But I do wish to point out the importance of this, and give you some practical application for your own website.

If you have studied marketing you are aware of AIDA. It's an acronym which describes a series of events that occur when a consumer engages with advertisement. It stands for Attention, Interest, Desire, and Action.

A You first need to attract the **attention** of a potential customer.

I Then you must raise customer **interest** by focusing on the benefits, and by demonstrating advantages they will receive.

D Next, when you show that you will satisfy the customer's needs, they begin to **desire** what you have to offer.

A And finally, you lead the customers toward taking **action** or purchasing what you have to offer.

There have been several variations of the AIDA theme put forth over the years, but the overall concept remains. Many times, when you arrive at a website and quickly realize you chose the wrong one, it's the result of the website failing to live up to AIDA.

It would be rather easy to argue that the three questions we looked at in Chapter 5 (where am I, what offer can I take advantage of, why should I choose you) are really just part of the attention phase of AIDA. In many cases that is true, so I could have rolled these two sections into one.

However, I prefer to keep them separate because I think of AIDA as more of a deliberate process of walking your website visitor through a series of steps designed to move them from arrival on your site to taking the action you want them to take.

In a sense, AIDA bridges the gap between establishing the orientation for the visitor and guiding them to the goals you are creating. It's the process that works both the conscious and subconscious mind to keep the visitors on your site moving in the right direction.

Therefore AIDA is important both from a macro view of the overall goal of your site, as well as the process of micro-conversions within a single page of your site. In fact, you can consider the steps of attention, interest, desire, and action each as their own micro-conversion. You grab attention, and convert that attention into interest. You expand upon that interest, and convert it into desire. You take that desire, and convert it into action. That action may convert to a click to the next page, or it may be the final action of submitting their email address or picking up the phone.

So what are some of the important elements you need on your pages to keep a visitor on track and move them through attention, interest, desire, and action without requiring them to think too much about it? Let's take a look.

Attention

The first, and most important element on any page, is the headline. We already looked at the title of a page because this shows up as the headline in the search results. But that title doesn't show within the context of your page. Of course you could make your page headline match the title, but usually the purpose is different so it's not always a good choice. The title, when it shows in search results, helps someone decide to click through to your site. Whereas headlines are important once someone arrives on the page because they grab attention, and they help the visitor decide if they are in the right place.

Basically, people use headlines on the page to help them decide whether or not to continue reading. If you lose them at the headline you have lost them. But if you win them at the headline they will go deeper into your site.

Your headline should be factual, but it must connect with your site visitors. To minimize disorientation, it should be consistent with what drew them into your site in the first place. Then it can grab their attention by using interesting words that are powerfully benefit-based and emotionally-driven. It must also set the tone, or match the tone, of what follows. Visually, headlines should also have a larger font size and sometimes a different font face or color so that they stand out from the other text on the page. You want your site visitors to be able to find your headline easily without scanning your page.

Here are some examples of attention grabbing headlines. The first from McDonald's, gets attention with the words in the headline as well as the isolated photo of the product.

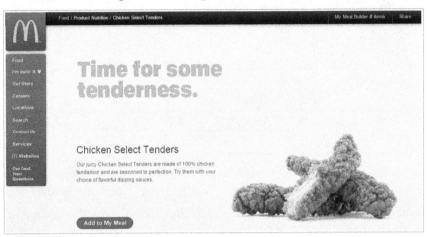

At Apple, they are going for simplicity. If you searched for the new Apple Watch, and landed on this page, your disorientation would be gone instantly.

Or, instead of looking at these major brands, we could look at a small online business. In the home page example on the next page, the photo and banner rotate out – with new headlines on the right side arriving every few seconds.

When someone clicks the "learn more" button below this headline, or if they do a search and land directly on the chocolate classes landing page, they would be greeted by the following page and a text-only headline.

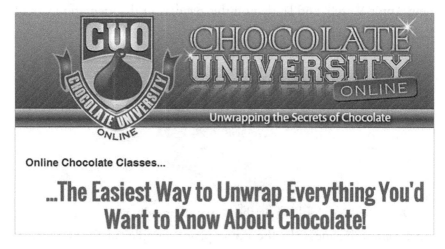

If you had searched for these things, would the headlines be strong enough to keep you on the page?

Interest

Now that the headline has held the visitor's attention, it's time to lock in their interest. This can often be accomplished by following the headline with some kind of subtle bribe. Tell the visitor what they can expect if they continue to read on. If you will be offering something free, mention right away the value they will receive. Your goal here is to capture their interest, and keep them moving through your process.

Take a look at this page from Apple.

Shot on iPhone 6

People take incredible photos and videos on iPhone 6 every day. And here are some of our favorites. Explore the gallery, learn a few tips, and see what's possible with the world's most popular camera.

Learn about iPhone 6 Camera ›

If you were looking for an iPhone 6 photo gallery, you are in the right place. And, if you stay around you will learn some tips and see what's possible. Does that keep your interest?

Another factor of holding on to the visitor's interest is to make the content on the page easy to look at. You do not want a visitor to struggle to find what they're looking for. Can anyone get lost on this Apple page? No way! The gallery is right there on the page. And if the visitor wants more information about the camera, the link is quite obvious.

It's pretty easy to understand that you want a headline to stand out from the text around it, but it's also effective to break long sections of text with section headers, other objects, or space. These elements not only help people skim the content to find the things that are most important for them, but they also increase overall readability on a page. Areas of too much text all crammed together can cause more eye fatigue and create feelings of being overwhelmed, two things that erode interest and send visitors away from your site.

Another important element in your arsenal is the bullet. Readers like bullet points because they are visually appealing, and are generally offset from the paragraph margins. They help readers quickly find information they seek. You can include important details at bullet points because they are likely to be noticed.

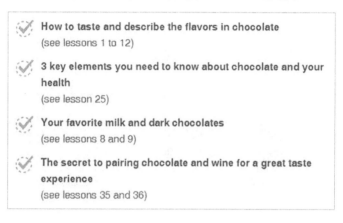

The last elements I will mention here are photos and videos. Most people are visually oriented, so any time you can include a picture that supports your message, you are strengthening that message.

Take a look at the image on the next page. This is the same Apple Watch page as used in the headline example a few pages back. The photo is quite interesting, as is the way it is presented.

In the headline example, I pulled out the headline and the links beneath it so that you could focus on the message. But looking at the larger page, the image really stands out. It helps grab your attention, and it certainly gets you interested in digging deeper. Only after you take in the photo, do you notice the headline. In this case, the headline also helps define the image. Then your eyes go right back to the picture, keeping you interested, and wanting more.

Videos are a powerful element too. In part, this is because they allow you to communicate directly, person to person. A recent study by Internet Retailer found that...

"52% of consumers who watch videos feel more confident about making purchases"

They also reported that people stop watching videos when the videos provide little information to help decision making. Yet 66% of viewers will watch information-heavy videos more than once.

It's also interesting to note that videos are not required to resemble a Hollywood production. Sometimes a simple video of a business slide-show presentation can be quite effective. Short bits of text changing on the screen, along with narration, can often keep visitors' interest longer than their own reading of the same text on the page. If you think about it, the static text keeps one of the visitors' senses engaged, while video and narration keep two senses active. That's twice the engagement for the same material.

At the top of the next page you will see an example of an embedded video from Starbucks. In this case the video is below the fold (that is, you have to scroll down the web page to see it). You are compelled to click because of the play button on the photo.

OUR COMMITMENT TO 100% ETHICALLY SOURCED COFFEE

For 15 years, we've worked with Conservation International to create a new way to buy coffee. One that's better for farmers, the planet, and coffee lovers everywhere.

Find out more »

Of course, integrating video into your business site might be more difficult than changing text, so you will have to check with your web developer. Once you have video in place, swapping it out to test different variations can be quite simple. If you are in a position to develop a new website, plan to keep some space available for video on key pages.

Desire

At this point you have kept visitors engaged, interested in what your site has to say. They are looking for more, but that doesn't mean they are ready to take the action you want them to take. Now it's time to ramp up their desire. There are several ways to accomplish this.

When you start presenting the content of your site, whether it's text, images, or video, be sure to include emotions that are similar in tone to your headline. Don't go overboard, but in a few sentences to a paragraph or two, communicate the full impact of the headline.

At Chocolate University Online, one of the headlines is **Immerse Yourself in the Feeling of Chocolate!** The following text begins a few lines below the headline.

> *How do you feel when you are eating chocolate? What if you could feel that way all the time?*

Then another paragraph, a little bit down the page, connects the visitors' feelings of chocolate with the business.

At Chocolate University Online we strive to give you the feeling of chocolate all the time. As a student, your mind will be focused on chocolate more than ever before. You will have more chocolate moments, and more enjoyment in those moments, as you gain insight into your favorite food.

The headline and the content of these paragraphs keep the reader in the same emotional place. One naturally flows into the next without disorienting the user or jerking them into a new frame of mind.

Also be sure to talk about, and to, the visitor/prospect. (You can test any web page with the customer focus calculator that I mentioned earlier, go to **www.customerfocuscalculator.com**.) Connect with whatever is going on in their mind. What emotions does the visitor have that would have brought him/her to seek out the solution your business offers? How is it that you can solve their problems? What are the benefits? Structurally, it can be effective to make each benefit a sub-header on the page, followed by two or three paragraphs of more detail. Or, to keep it shorter, a bullet list of benefits can also work well.

As you put this all together, remember your visitor's internal credibility sensor. Theoretically if you're bringing in appropriate emotions, tied to a headline that already hooked them, and giving the benefits they are looking for, you are not likely to lose the visitor on the boredom side of the equation. But you still risk the problem of disbelief. This means you have to convince the visitor that what you have said is true.

To do this, you must appeal directly to their credibility sensor. Wherever it makes sense in the flow, include useful statistics, expert endorsements, customer testimonials. Each of these elements help to prove that you can deliver the benefits or results that you promise. As doubt decreases, desire increases.

> *"Chocolate University lessons are the best. Not only am I learning interesting and helpful information but the chocolate labs & weekly assignments are delicious! P.S. They're really lots of fun too."*

- Sue, in Yuma, Arizona

Action

When desire has reached its peak, it's time to offer an action step. Sometimes the A-I-D is subtle because all you have is a micro-conversion goal. The action you want may be as simple as a click to another page. But if this is your sales page, where you are attempting to close the final deal, then the action you seek represents the ultimate goal of your site.

Make the offer you intend to make, and repeat the benefit shown in the headline. If this initial benefit was strong enough to keep the visitors' attention in the beginning, then it's important to them. Also allude to the other benefits along the way. It may have been one or more of the other benefits that that helped carry the visitor to this final action point.

Microsoft has a page called "Why Windows". They first grab the visitors' attention with a bold photograph and a related title.

Creators are powered by Windows

Josh Henderson is part visionary, part food entrepreneur. With the help of Windows, working across all his devices, he transformed the street food scene in Seattle and opened three restaurants of his own.

Below this section of the page they give the real title, **Seven reasons to choose Windows**. This title tells you that you're in the right place. Then the page has seven large sections with images and a description in each part. If staying connected, no matter what device you are using, is important to you, then reason number 5, "Always Connected" will really ramp up your desire. By the time you get to reason number 7 you are ready for more.

So what comes immediately after this photo? A variety of action steps that the visitor can take next; more exploration as well as shopping opportunities if they are ready to buy.

None of these action steps are direct purchase steps, but all complete the goal of this page and move the visitor into the next step in the sales process, whichever step is right for the visitor.

It's here in the Action step that you have to justify the "price." What that price is, depends on your goal.

If the goal is a micro-conversion, to move the user to the next step, the price is low. It is the effort of a minor decision and a click.

Of course, if you are selling a product or service there is an actual monetary price. Did everything up to this point create enough value so that the visitor can decide to complete the purchase?

If the goal is to capture an email address as a lead, there's still a price, a rather high price. The visitor is concerned that they will get unrelenting spam. Can you justify that perceived cost? Or can you minimize that price in the visitor's mind?

It's similar if you want the visitor to pick up the phone and call you. They may be concerned about your sales process or even the functioning of your phone system. They don't know what will happen the moment after they dial your number. And for some people that is a high price. What can you say or do on your website that minimizes this price, this anxiety?

Here's an example, that goes from attention to action all within a small area at the top of a potential landing page.

If you were looking to solve a bed bug problem, the headline proves you are in the right place. There are two offers. One shows a discount to help increase your interest. And the other goes for action. The action seeks to give you a choice in the method that helps you feel the most comfortable. In other words, you can choose the method that has the lowest response cost for you. You can call with the phone number at the top or you can fill in the FREE Estimate Now box if you view that as easier.

There is one more way to help encourage action from your visitors. What can you do to reverse their risk? If a visitor is making an actual purchase, can you present some kind of guarantee? You want them to take action, so how can you assure the prospect that he or she has nothing to lose by taking this action with your business right now? These are important questions, so I'll spend some time on this idea in the next chapter.

CHAPTER 7 – KEY POINTS TO REMEMBER

Apply the lessons of direct response marketing to your website:

- **Attention**: The first, and most important element on any page is the headline.

- **Interest**: Tell visitors what they can expect if they stay on the page. Be sure your message is easy to understand.

- **Desire**: Communicate the full impact of the headline. Be credible – as doubt decreases, desire increases.

- **Action**: Make the offer you intend to make and repeat the most significant benefits.

Want help applying AIDA to your website? The workbook includes a landing page outline showing you how to implement each step. Do that now. If you don't have the workbook, you can still get it at: **www.dominatethetop.com/workbook**.

CHAPTER 8
COMPONENT #6 – TRUST ELEMENTS

The relationship with your website visitors will be extremely short if they do not trust your business or your message. The good news, when visitors find your site through a Google search and have never heard of your business before, is that they don't already mistrust you. At the same time, they have no trust either, and they may be quite skeptical. As we've already seen, their credibility sensor is likely on high alert.

In order to move new visitors to take the action you seek, you must start building trust. There are some specific elements you can include in your website that will help your visitors trust you and your business more than others. Isn't it true that everyone, given a choice, would rather transact business with those they trust? And if they trust you more than your competition you are much more likely to gain the customers.

Only after a visitor believes that they know, like, and trust your business will they take any action. Of course there are some exceptions to this. For example, if the prospect is looking for a specific product which you happen to sell at a better price than your competition, they might not be too concerned about knowing and liking you if the relationship is young. They may use this first purchase as an opportunity to find out. But they still must have some level of trust before they will go forward with a transaction. They are asking themselves questions such as, "will you deliver on time," "will you accept returns if it doesn't work," "is there someone to talk to if there's a problem?" All of these are issues you have to address if you want to build a good level of trust quickly.

Any time someone makes a purchase, or provides their email, or picks up the phone, there is some degree of risk on the part of the buyer. And the less they know you, trust you, and like you, the greater their perception of that risk.

Let's take a look at four things you can do to build trust in a short amount of time. These are testimonials, guarantees, contact information, and third-party validation.

Testimonials

Testimonials and reviews can be quite powerful when worked into your website. I will make a quick distinction between a testimonial and a review. Both are accounts of your business, products or services from the perspective of a client or customer. I view testimonials as short and focused on benefits or results for the user. Reviews are generally longer, and often focus on features of the product or service.

You may benefit with both testimonials and reviews on your site. Detailed reviews are an excellent partner with product and service descriptions. However, in this chapter I am concentrating on testimonials. Testimonials are more concise and, when used properly, can be most effective in building overall trust for your business. They are also more versatile because the credibility of one testimonial can often apply to your entire business.

Good testimonials always generate a positive impact because of one very important factor – social proof. Social proof is a psychological concept where people will follow the lead of others who they believe are acting appropriately. In general, social proof helps us know how to behave correctly when we have no previous experience. We can watch others who we believe know the correct action or response. If others are doing something, that's validation it's OK for me to do the same thing.

Many visitors to your website will not be familiar with your business. Having testimonials helps them understand how others have experienced your business in the past. Since the testimonials come from knowledgeable users of your business, it provides some of the social validation that you are looking for.

Any testimonial from a real customer is better than no testimonial at all, but I prefer a specific structure that packs a lot of power into three sentences.

- The first sentence tells the problem someone had before engaging with your company.
- The second sentence tells how your business solved the problem for them.
- The third sentence tells the results they achieved. Straight-forward and to the point.

This structure works well because the visitors arriving at your site likely have the same or similar problems. That's why they were searching in the first place. When they arrive at your site and see a testimonial from someone else, they can identify with the other customer.

The first sentence connects them with the problem they are already having. The second sentence then reinforces their desire. They lock in with the credibility, wanting to have much the same experience as the person who gave the testimonial. The third sentence seals the deal. It's showing the results the first person got. The visitor to your site definitely wants those results!

Besides the power of social proof, there's another benefit to you and your website with this testimonial structure. A testimonial that is three sentences long is short enough to include anywhere on your website. That means you can start to include them everywhere that it makes sense, on any page, next to any product or service.

So how do you get these testimonials? First, ask those who are already regular customers that feel good about your business. They might be willing to write up something for you real quick. Another way is to engage one of your customers in conversation and then ask them if you could get some feedback from them.

Assuming they agree, ask a simple question like, "hey, before you bought this service or that product what problem were you having?" Make a note of their answer. Then ask, "and how did we help you solve that problem?" Make a note of this. And finally ask, "so what happened next? Clearly you have come back to us, so we must have solved your problem. What kind of result or benefit did you receive?"

The worst case scenario is that you have learned something nice about your business. But better yet, you can take those three answers and write them up into a testimonial. Here is the most important step: **You write the testimonial into three sentences for your customer.** You could ask your customer to do it, but most likely they will put it off. They might not want to take the time, or they may be self-conscious about what they would write, or perhaps they simply don't like the idea of writing, or they have some other reason why they can't get to it. When you write the testimonial for them, those excuses go away.

Then, the next time you see this customer, or have an opportunity to call or email, ask if you captured the information accurately and if you could publish this on your website as a testimonial? If they agree, also ask if you can use their name or even name and city. If they hesitate, say you won't use their last name. Of course having their full name and city is best as your prospects will be more inclined to understand the validity of the claim. That's because we believe that...

If someone is willing to be identified, what they said must certainly be true.

I want to caution you against fake testimonials. In the U.S., the FTC (Federal Trade Commission) enforces the rules for what is allowed to be said online. True unrewarded testimonials are valid. If you must compensate someone to provide a testimonial, that has to be disclosed. And if someone makes a claim that is unusual, that must also be disclosed. (You've seen that before on TV ads saying "results not typical." It's that kind of thing.)

Here's an example testimonial. "Our website was generating an average of about $450 per month sales until I read Jeff's book. We implemented all of the website fixes that were presented in the book. Now business is booming with our monthly web sales exceeding $450,000." If I wrote this testimonial and put it on our website just because I wanted to, it would be fake, morally wrong, and the FTC could shut us down.

On the other hand, if you provided me with this testimonial as truthful, I would love to show this. But I would have to disclose that these results are not typical. While I can imagine that these kind of results are possible for some businesses in some situations, a thousand-fold improvement based on reading a book, doesn't really pass the sniff test. Most people will make incremental improvements, not such a vast transformation. The results might be based more on the action of the student than on the influence of the teacher. Or the results might have happened coincidentally because of various environmental circumstances for the business. Yet, if it is true, I want to display it because, presumably, my book contributed to their success.

However, if I were to start receiving similar claims regularly, then the results would be considered as typical, and I would be able to legitimately brag about it as such.

My point is that it's best to be careful where claims are concerned. If they can be viewed as deceptive then you have a problem. Keep them real and focused on the results that someone has already experienced with your business, and you have a winning edge in the trust department. (I am not a lawyer. Please do not consider this statement about testimonial usage as legal advice. The FTC has strict rules that continue to evolve. Please consult your own attorney and see **www.ftc.gov** for more information.)

If you have never included testimonials on your website before, or you just have a few weak ones, use the three question formula. Once you have a few, you might want to expand the questioning to get deeper, more meaningful responses. That's more of an advanced topic so I pulled it out of this book. However, I am making a copy of this additional formula available to you so that you have it for later reference. As soon as you are ready, you can get access at **www.dominatethetop.com/bonus**.

Now work out how you are going to collect some of these important testimonials and where you want to put them within your site.

Guarantees

Before trust is truly built and solidifies, your prospects are perceiving some form of risk in dealing with you. Therefore, guarantees can serve to reverse that risk. A meaningful guarantee will take the risk upon your business, moving it away from your prospect so that they are more comfortable to move forward.

What's a meaningful guarantee? It's one that is easily understood which doesn't create new risks.

Here's a poor guarantee. It is real. Let's say this is from Department Store One...

"We promise to attempt a return on every item purchased in our stores.

"Most unopened items in new condition returned within 90 days will receive a refund or exchange. Items that are opened or damaged or do not have a packing slip or receipt may be denied a refund or exchange."

This is not a good guarantee from the customer perspective. It doesn't truly reverse the risks. Actually, this guarantee might have good intent, but as a consumer I don't know for sure. For example, what if I buy something that must be opened before I know if I like it, am I protected in the return or not?

It sounds to me that if I buy something from this store, and I don't like it once I've tried it, I might be stuck with it anyway. What happens if the item works as it is supposed to, but I don't like the quality? Am I entitled to a refund? The way I read this, the answer is no.

Here's another real guarantee. Let's say this is from Department Store Two...

"If you bought something at one of our stores and need to return or exchange it, you can take it back to any of our stores, not just the one where it was purchased.

"For most items, we accept returns within 90 days after purchase. Here's how to return your item to a store:
- Bring the item you wish to return to the Customer Service desk.
- Be sure to also bring all original packing materials and accessories.
- If available, bring the receipt that came with the item."

With the second store, I can buy something at one store, take it out of the package, try it out, decide I don't like it, grab the packing materials, and take it to another store. I don't even have to search for my receipt or repackage it. That's solid.

Now let's say that these two stores are roughly the same distance from my house, and the item I want to buy is at both of them for approximately the same price. Which store would I choose to shop at? Certainly Department Store Two because they are holding onto the risk. They are assuring me that if I'm not satisfied for any reason, then they've got my back. They will make it right.

This is a factor that can separate many businesses. In the online world, where your business can be quickly evaluated against your competition, you have to have the strongest guarantee, the best risk reversal.

If you can offer a 100% money-back guarantee with no questions asked, that's top of the line. How about this example from an online retailer:

> *"If you are not 100% satisfied with your purchase, you can return your order to the warehouse for a full refund.*
>
> *"We believe that in order to have the best possible online shopping experience, our customers should not have to pay for domestic return shipping.*
>
> *"So if for whatever reason you're not happy with your purchase, just go through our easy self-service return process to print out a free return label - your domestic shipping costs are prepaid.*
>
> *"With our 365 day return policy, there are no special catches or exceptions. All we ask is that you send the items back to us in the original packaging, and make sure that the merchandise is in the same condition."*

Nice, huh? Within the fine print, they go on to say,

"You can return your purchase for up to 365 days from the purchase date.

"If you purchase on 2/29 of a Leap Year, then you have until 2/29 the following Leap Year to return those orders. That's four whole years!"

They could have said, "you have until March 1 the following year," but they didn't. They gave you until the same date in the future. In this case they are strengthening the guarantee with the details rather than making moves that give the risks back to the buyer.

How can you do something like this? The other important lesson in this internet retailer's guarantee is the time period of 365 days, one year.

Studies have shown that the longer you make your guarantee period, the fewer returns you get. Though this seems a little counter-intuitive, the logic is sound.

Let's say you buy something and have 7 days in which to return it. You are going to test it out and make sure it is perfect. If any questions remain in your mind toward the end of that week you likely return it. If the guarantee is 30 days, you make a note in your calendar or reminder system at around day 28 so you can decide whether to return it or not.

If the guarantee is a year, you may also make a note to remind yourself, but by then you have been using the product or service. Whether you like it or not is irrelevant. You feel you have been given a fair chance to use it, and you have been using it. Therefore your purchase is justified, even if the first month was frustrating because it didn't work as well as you had hoped.

Frankly, there's also a large percentage of purchasers who never remind themselves, but they maintain in memory that they have 7 days or they have a month. The person who will hold onto the return date in their head for a year would be quite rare. So someone could decide on day 6 to return an item. If the return date is day 7 they do it, they return the item.

If the return date is day 30, they say to themselves, "I can do it next week or the week after when it's convenient." Some do the return, and some don't. Some returns will fall through the cracks, simply because more time has elapsed.

With a 365 day return policy, they think, "oh there's no hurry, I can return it any time." And as time goes on the return becomes less and less important.

While all that is backed up by research, there is still a persistent fear among businesses that if they make the return policy completely risk-free, many people will take advantage of them.

If you have a good product or service you don't really have to worry about this. People are not usually buying something with the intent to return. They are buying with the intent to solve the problem that faces them.

Full 60-day Money Back Guarantee

Purchases of Chocolate University Online classes are through Clickbank, a trusted online retailer. This offers added security for you. One of the rules I have to follow to work with them is that I've got to offer you a 60-day, money-back guarantee. That's OK with me. I stand behind my materials completely and know you'll be completely thrilled with the content and, more importantly, the knowledge you've gained.

In case you need it, for your peace of mind, know that a refund is available anytime for the next 60 days by simply emailing me or Clickbank if you are dissatisfied for any reason.

Will a strong guarantee result in more returns than if you had a weak guarantee? Yes, most likely it will. But consider that a great risk reversal could add 20% more customers, while your returns rate picks up by 1 or 2 percent. That's a major improvement to your bottom line.

Another way to look at this is that a poor guarantee means you will lose sales that you could have otherwise had. You are giving up part of your potential market. Whereas a great guarantee means you reach all the sales you should have, and you also get more questionable buyers to try out your business. You will lock in more of them, but yes, some of them may not be a good match for your business. It's mutually better if they are not your customer, so you give them their money back, and they can move on. Without the strong guarantee, you would have never sold to them in the first place. Since you likely don't want to deal with them long-term, give them their money back. You are really only returning money to a portion of those people who became your customer only due to the great guarantee.

Therefore the guarantee does not create a loss, it extends your margin of victory. And these refunds might even create a story of trust which helps these same people purchase happily in the future, or refer their friends who are a better fit for your business.

Please think seriously about how you can improve your guarantee. It will make a difference for your business, especially in the online world.

Contact Information

When you visit a new website and you are interested in buying something from that business, but you can find no telephone number, what do you think? Most people will think that the business does not want to be contacted. If that's the case, what if there is a problem with the purchase? If there's no one to talk to before you buy, how will you resolve any issues after you buy? This is why contact information is so important. Its presence helps build trust.

Providing a variety of contact methods makes it easier for your site visitors to contact you. It's all about making them comfortable enough to engage with your business even though they hardly know you.

The first thing to consider is your phone number. When someone new arrives on your site, they don't know anything about your business. For some, it's important that you have a phone number where they can call you. That doesn't mean they will call, but the phone number implies that you have a real business with someone who can actually answer the phone.

Your prospects and customers believe that by seeing a phone number, it means they CAN call IF they have questions or problems. Therefore the phone number is important whether they ever use it or not.

To raise your credibility further, offer a toll-free number. For many people, it doesn't matter whether they call an area code or 1-800, it costs them nothing extra with their calling plan anyway. But, by having a toll free number, you are saying that you want to be easily available, so much so that you're willing to pay for someone to call you. It's a nice gesture, and it gets noticed relative to your competition. Of course the impact will vary by industry.

These days, if you include a toll-free number, you should also include your local number. The local number strengthens the bond for those in your area. This is especially important if you have a storefront. Some people are also more comfortable calling a local phone number because they believe that the call will be answered at the business itself, whereas a toll-free number might be a call center.

The local phone number is also an important consideration for Google. As the search engine increases the importance of local search, which they have been doing over the past few years, they cross-reference your address and phone number with other online sources to boost your business's credibility within the local results.

The next aspect of your phone number is the consideration of where it should be placed on your website. The answer is everywhere.

If someone wants to call you, do you want them to have to look for your phone number? If a method of contact is not obvious, they might decide to search for another company rather than digging for your number on some obscure page. Of course this depends on your business model. If you really don't want people to call, then you can make it a little less visible. But in most cases, if you are selling a product or service, and you want to speed up the process from prospect to customer, it's a good idea to show your phone number. The best place is typically in the upper right of every page. People are conditioned to look there.

It's also good to include your phone number at the bottom of your pages, in the footer section, possibly along with your physical address, if appropriate. And, certainly, the phone number belongs on your Contact Us page.

While people like to see a phone number, the reality is that if they're online, they might want to stay online. Regardless of the time of day, they might want to reach out to your business, and they don't need an instant response. The contact form helps solve this problem.

What belongs on a contact form? You have seen those forms that ask for your name, address, home phone number, business phone number, cell phone number, which product you own, what operating system it runs on, your favorite color, the barometric pressure, your children's names, ethnic heritage, shoe size, and finally your question for support. On top of all that, they make all the form fields mandatory. Egad! If you're like me, you've started filling out such a form and then quit before ever submitting.

A simple form is always best. The fewer form fields you have, the more likely a visitor will take the time to fill it out. Name, email address, and a question box are generally all you need. You might want to give the option for them to provide a phone number. This way, if they provide it, you can call them back. That can be perceived as a higher level of customer service. Once the conversation is started, whether in email or over the phone, you can ask questions to get the additional information that you will need to properly address the concerns. If you ask every conceivable question up front, it might save you some time later, but you will have reduced your potential audience in the process.

Providing a contact email address is also a good idea. If you represent a larger company, you might consider a contact directory instead of a single address. But don't go overboard. A large email directory can be confusing for someone to figure out who they should contact. Therefore it's good to reference a single point of contact. You could say, "For specific questions refer to the email listing by department below. For general questions, or if you don't know which department to contact, send your email to sales@ourbusiness.com." In this case you must ensure that someone monitors the general address and follows up or forwards to the appropriate person in your company.

With the explosion of social media, online shoppers enjoy the added level of contact that becomes available when a business takes advantage of social methods. The biggest and most popular, especially in the business to consumer arena, is Facebook. If your business has a Facebook page, then include a link to that page wherever appropriate. At a minimum include the link to your Facebook page on your contact page. If you can, it's OK to include the link on every page of your site as well. A small Facebook icon is sufficient.

Also, consider using Facebook even if your company sells to other businesses. Decisions are made by people in those businesses, and many of those people use Facebook. At this point, you ought to have a presence there regardless of your business.

One of the reasons that Facebook is important is that people believe that interacting with a business is most easily accomplished through the business Facebook page, as if there is some magic to the way Facebook works. Why not feed that perception? If people want to interact with your business, and they want to use Facebook to do it, help them find your business there.

Some businesses can also benefit with a Twitter account. If you have one, include the Twitter logo icon next to the Facebook logo icon throughout your site. The same holds true for LinkedIn. If you have a LinkedIn business page, you should include that link as well.

Your customers have different preferences. So implement as many of these as you are comfortable using. Theoretically, the more, the better. You are more likely to reach different people with varied communication methods. However, you must also be realistic with your time. I believe it is better to pick one and be well-represented there than to be poorly-represented everywhere. Start with the platform that is likely to have the greatest impact for your business.

One final location within your site, where contact information becomes important, is in the checkout process. If you have an ecommerce store, and several steps to check out, you must make the process as simple as possible for your customers. Part of that process is making sure they can reach you if they need help. For many businesses a large percentage of people who start the checkout process never finish. This is called *shopping cart abandonment*.

Shopping cart abandonment doesn't happen as often in the physical world. It's rare for someone to go through a store, filling up their cart with the things they want only to push the cart off to the side and walk out of the store.

I'm sure you've had questions arise while shopping. Perhaps you can't find what you're looking for, whether a specific product or the advertised special. Or you need an explanation as to why this one is on sale and that one isn't. What do you do in these cases? Typically, you find someone who can help you. Sometimes employees are walking around. They might see your puzzled look and ask you if you need help. Other times you have to seek someone out. You get help.

You get your questions answered, and you proceed to make your purchase, perhaps setting one product aside if it turns out to not be right.

But online, people get stuck, find there's no one to talk to, and then just walk away, not purchasing anything. Why is that?

The entire process becomes too much for them
if they have to search for an answer.

They would rather start over with another merchant than work to get answers. So make the communication easy for them. Include your phone number on every page. Include frequently asked questions with good answers. Include shipping details and pricing, because that's a big area of concern that causes abandonment.

If you can swing it, go for the internet's closest equivalent to the helpful store assistant. That is the live chat box. Even if you don't have an ecommerce site, live chat can be another helpful way to increase engagement with your site visitors and move them along toward your sale. They can chat with someone in real time to get their questions answered without even having to pick up the phone. It's very convenient.

Providing a variety of contact methods is a demonstration of your customer service. You are offering customers multiple ways to get answers, using their telephone or using their computer. Having these options right in the checkout process, rather than just on a Contact Us page will make a big difference in your ability to complete online sales.

I have already brought up the Web Genius Summit that I put together a few years ago. One of the featured experts was Audrey Kerwood. She went over eight things that are necessary in order to get the best conversion possible in ecommerce sites. If you have an online store, you must include each of these eight things. And, they are also good to consider even if you don't have an online store. As with other extras, this list is included in the bonus material at **www.dominatethetop.com/bonus**.

Now take a moment to review the pages of your website. What contact information do you have now? What changes should you make?

Third-Party Validation

As we become more isolated from each other because of technology, we also seek to be more connected using technology. Rather than the old person-to-person word of mouth, we resort to other means of gathering proof that a business is worth dealing with.

As I mentioned earlier, seeing or listening to testimonials is one of the ways we find validation. We can get a feeling for how someone else did with the company, product, or service. If we can relate to the comments, we start to get the proof we need.

> *Everyone else was swimming naked in the piranha infested waters, so I thought it would be a good idea too.*

It is natural for people to want proof that your site is telling the truth on whatever subject the visitor is interested in. If someone believes you are not telling the truth, they will not trust you, and you will not get their business. On the other hand, once you establish trust, progress can follow.

Begin by offering some reassurance to your visitors. You can accomplish this by including various forms of third-party validation. Testimonials are good, but they are only one such method of validation. There are others that can also be used to strengthen your message.

Some of these methods date back to offline practices; for example, displaying the logos of other businesses. It can be helpful to show who else you have done business for. If a prospect is on your site and discovers that you have provided products or services to a business the visitor already respects, that goes a long way to helping build trust.

Another element that you often see on websites are various industry seals. If your business is a member of a trade organization and they allow you to include their logo or emblem, do it. That gives you credibility which creates trust. If your business is a member of the Better Business Bureau or a local Chamber of Commerce, make that known as well. These types of organizations may not specifically vouch for your business, but the membership is perceived to be selective since not every business can claim membership.

Social proof is another aspect of third-party validation. It's this type of evidence that has helped Facebook to become so popular, especially in the way consumers think of using Facebook as a good way to deal with a business. They can see the interaction on the business page and determine that your business is legitimate and that it cares. They can see how the existing customers comment and question. They can imagine how they themselves fit into the picture. This builds up their trust through the social aspects of the site. It gives them some of the social proof they are looking for.

Basically in our human nature we want to know that we are making good decisions, so we, in part, make decisions based on how others have made decisions in the past. This helps speed up our decision making process. If we believe that someone else has already considered the pros and cons, and made a decision accordingly, then we can expend much less energy by simply following the path they have already chosen. Plus, to look at the darker side of human nature, it also gives us an excuse if something goes wrong. To follow up on the observation, "Everyone else was swimming naked in the piranha infested waters, so I thought it would be a good idea too," the swimmer might deflect the blame saying, "Darn everyone else, I wanted to keep that appendage!"

Another form of validation is accomplished through various technology seals. You have likely seen secure website logos that confirm that all transactions are encrypted. Some seals claim that a website is verified to be virus free. Others claim that the business has taken some positive action to help the visitors in some way.

Most of these seals come with a cost. Whether they are worthwhile for your business will depend on your audience. What do they think of the importance? When I wrote about defining your page goals I mentioned a testing method called a split test. Details of this topic are coming up later, but I want to mention that the decision to use these seals or not can be a good subject for a split test. If the test results show that conversion is boosted enough to cover the cost, then you would want to continue ongoing use of these types of seals.

One of the seals that I personally use on many sites provides a subtle social proof along with helpful buying information for site visitors. This one is called the HonestE Super-Seal.

When it is embedded on a website, it shows the current date and suggests that the visitor click to verify before they buy. When a visitor clicks, they see contact information for the business, find some important rules for shopping online, and get to review the pledge that the member business has made as part of the HonestE membership requirements.

The most important part of the HonestE program is that the site lets you put your business out there, where others can make their complaints public. As a merchant you get to respond. If you do so in a timely manner, all is well. But if you don't, then prospects can view this information.

Using a service like this is clearly not a good idea unless you run an honest business with the true intent to take care of your customers. And that's the point. Most of us want to run legitimate businesses. By using a service like this we're saying "here's the proof, no complaints!" Assuming your business is meant to take care of customers in some way, then this type of seal might serve your business well, especially since experimentation has shown a boost of up to 17% in conversion rates. Of course, your mileage may vary. (You can get a free account here: **www.honestylogo.com**.)

About Us Page

There is another page of your website that can help build trust and credibility for your business. It is the About Us page. On many websites this page is among the top most visited pages. Yet the About Us page is often thrown together quickly, or overlooked completely, in favor of the products and services that the business offers.

You have already seen the importance of focusing your website on your visitors. When someone arrives they want your site to answer their pressing concerns. But the time may come when your visitors want to know more about the business they are dealing with. An About Us page is your chance to turn the focus back onto your business. If someone chooses to go to that page, they expect to learn about you. They expect that this page is more about your business than it is about them.

The About Us page is your chance to sell the visitor on your business, not on a specific product or service, but on your business as a whole. This page should help demonstrate to the visitor what your company can do for them. Give examples of how your business has helped others in the past. Even though this page is about your business, the visitors still have their own needs in mind. It's about making a connection that the visitor can understand and, therefore, trust.

The About Us page should also be fact-based. The temptation is to fill this page with many of those "unhearable" words I mentioned in Chapter 5. If you choose to say that your business is the "leading provider of xyz" or that "it's your people that make the difference" your visitors will stop. They don't need cliches or even your opinion. For best results present verifiable facts. If you can show numbers, do that. People love them and believe them. Belief leads to credibility and more trust.

While fact-based information is excellent, providing too much can detract from your message. For example, a detailed explanation about every year of your history, with links to every press release, and discussion of each and every change that occurred within the organization, is over the top. No one needs that much detail in order to decide to hire your firm or make a purchase.

To summarize, what do your prospects typically want to know about your business to help them decide that choosing you would be a smart move? That's what belongs on this page of your site.

Google Quality Score

Besides the trust elements that we have already explored, there are a few other pages that have the potential to help you get more traffic to your website. These are your privacy policy, terms of service, and a page for disclaimers. In reality, these pages are rarely visited by your human visitors unless they have a specific question.

However, it is generally believed that Google looks for the presence of these pages within a site. If they appear, your site is considered more credible, possibly to the point of having a higher "quality score" than sites that do not have these pages. The Google quality score has a direct impact on your site if you use Google advertising. Higher quality scores can achieve higher rank positions at lower cost.

Here are excerpts in Google's own words. Within a section titled, "How we calculate Quality Score" one of the bullet points says, "The quality of your landing page: How relevant, transparent, and easy-to-navigate your page is."

To expand on that we can navigate to another of Google's support pages titled, "Understanding landing page experience." On this page it says:

> "Landing page experience refers to how good we think someone's experience will be when they get to your landing page (the web page they end up on after clicking your ad). You can improve your landing page experience by:
>
> • providing relevant, useful, and original content,
>
> • promoting transparency and fostering trustworthiness on your site (for example, by explaining your products or services before asking visitors to fill out forms sharing their own information), and
>
> • making it easy for customers to navigate your site (including on mobile sites)."

Farther down that same page each of those bullet points are expanded. The section titled, "Transparency and trustworthiness" includes a bullet that says, "If you request personal information from customers, make it clear why you're asking for it and what you'll do with it." Therefore, by providing such details as privacy policies, disclaimers, and terms of service, you are increasing trustworthiness, at least according to Google.

And if Google sees these elements as higher quality for their advertising product, it doesn't take much of a leap to assume these same factors could come into play as indicators of search quality as well. If these pages will help Google trust your site, then they are worth including even if they are rarely ever used by your site visitors.

Chapter 8 – Key Points To Remember

Your site visitors prefer to do business with people they know, like, and trust.

Use testimonials and other third-party validation to help your visitors understand your business credibility.

Use strong guarantees to extend your margin of victory into the group of prospects who would have never purchased otherwise.

Make it easy for your customers and prospects to reach your business using the communication methods that serve them best.

Use verifiable facts on your About Us page to demonstrate legitimacy.

Other important pages of your site include your Privacy Policy, Terms of Service, and Disclaimers.

Go to the workbook now to review each of the trust elements for your site. If you don't have the workbook, you can get a copy from **www.dominatethetop.com/workbook**.

CHAPTER 9
COMPONENT #7 – VISUAL ENGAGEMENT

The final component of an effective website that I will cover in this book is visual engagement. What I mean by this is your use of color, images, and video.

Color is one of those things that can be part of the first impression a visitor gets within milliseconds of clicking to your website. Certainly there are times when you have seen a page and said, "yikes, who picked those colors." Yet often the impression made can be much more subtle, subconscious, or nearly so. Meanwhile the images and videos chosen for a page help to steer the engagement while communicating part of your message. They can help get attention and move a user toward action.

Once again you have to keep in mind your goals, and refer back to the keyword research you did when you started. Images and video will be much more effective if they connect both to your prospects inner conversation and your desired outcome.

Color Use

What I want to mention on the subject is that your use of color, especially color combinations, can increase or decrease the amount of time someone will spend on your site. Your website must be easy to read, easy on the eyes, and provide a good flow of information.

Color can help do this. In areas of text, you can create the best readability by having a darker font on a lighter background. That's not to say that you cannot flip that into light text on a dark background. But if you have lots of text, the reversed combination can lead to greater eye fatigue while reading. That can mean that a visitor becomes just a little bit more agitated, perhaps only subconsciously, but that might be enough to end the visit.

On the other hand, smaller areas of bold color, with light text, can draw attention. So the use of color backgrounds and font colors may be something you want to experiment with. You might even discover that a page that is slightly more difficult to read might have an appeal with your target audience precisely because of the overall look of the page. Only testing can reveal this to be true or not.

The second consideration of color is its relationship to your corporate identity. Marketing is always most effective when it can work together. I have often seen websites that do not follow the identity that a business has established offline. Sometimes this can make sense, for example when a business is rebranding, and their initial rollout is online followed by carrying the new identity through the rest of their company and collateral materials. However, it's more often that a business wants to have a certain appeal online, and they hire someone to develop their site without giving much thought to coordinating their identity. Sure, they get the same logo to work, but that seems like the only element that connects their worlds. If you are looking at your website critically right now, take a look at how well it integrates your overall marketing message. Start with color and move out to your vision, mission, values, culture, and so on.

The final point I will offer on color is that testing different colors in key positions can be a worthwhile effort. A number of years ago a study, published by a company called Performable (since acquired by HubSpot), showed that simply changing a call-to-action button from green to red resulted in a 21% increase in conversions. That's not to say that you should change all your buttons to red. What this means is that color matters, and you should experiment with different colors to see if there is one that makes a significant difference on your website.

That's really all I want to say about color. There are books available on color psychology so I will let you pursue that on your own in much more depth if you're interested. The key point here is that you ought to go after the best color scheme for your audience, not only the colors that look best to you.

Images

"A picture is worth a thousand words" is just as true online as off. The right image can be an eye-grabber that gets attention and helps focus your site's visitors on the issues you want them to focus on.

I am not a graphic designer. Those who are can create powerful images that will help connect your site's visitors to your message. The important point is that you have to have a message–a page goal–<u>before</u> you select or create an image. The images and graphic designs must support your messages and goals.

Images are so important to your website that Google weighs in on the subject even though the content of images does not impact your search rank. Part of the reason that Google cares about images is that Google offers its own image search options. (If you have never been there, take a look at **images.google.com**.) So, Google is biased toward making their own image search product better, but the suggestions they make also represent enhancements you can make to your own website.

For example, Google points out that you should "avoid embedding important text in images for elements like page headings and menu items because not all users can access them. To ensure maximum accessibility of your important text based content, keep it in regular HTML."

There are several important design points in those two sentences. The first point is to keep text out of images. This is a good idea if you want all visitors to get the same message. Some viewers will turn off all images. And, some sites are responsive, meaning they show up differently on mobile devices. Responsive sites may move and resize images to fit better. If those images contain key text, your users might not get the experience you intended. If your headlines or menu items are images of words, they could be missed.

The second point, which is really the flip side of the first, is to keep your important text in regular HTML. To put it simply, keep text as some form of text. Not only does this help ensure that everyone gets the same experience, but it also means that Google can read the content. This is especially important in headlines and menu items that help define the relevance of your site to the searcher's request. You want Google to be able to read these because they help with the search engine optimization of your site.

I hope it is clear that critical text should not be included in images. But then, does that mean images are completely worthless for SEO? No, there are some things you can do to get a boost from the images.

First, Google says you should give your images "informative filenames" because that can offer "clues about the subject matter of the image." They go on to say, "If we're unable to find suitable text in the page on which we found the image, we'll use the filename as the image's snippet in our search results." This refers to their image search again. It indicates that if there is suitable text on the page that can be used to describe the image, they will make that available to the searcher. But if that information is not there, then the file name of the image will work.

```
<img src="golf-clubs.jpg" alt="">
```

In the HTML code fragment above, the file name is golf-clubs.jpg. That provides some value to Google. It describes the photo. It is better than img0541.jpg that might come from your digital camera, but not as good as callaway-XR-pro-fairway-woods.jpg.

Next, Google points out the effective use of the "alt" attribute to describe an image. The "alt" attribute is a section in the HTML code of your website. This is a part of the code that has been abused by search engine optimizers in the past because it was an effective way to get extra unseen keywords in a page. Stuffing keywords in the alt attribute is no longer effective, in part because you want that space to define what the image really is. Restating your keyword phrase doesn't help define the image to the searcher unless, of course, the image is actually a picture of the item in your keyword phrase. Furthermore, in the case that a user has images turned off, or has a site read to them, the "alt" attributes provide the fill-in text.

To demonstrate this, take another look at the image tag above. It contains an alt attribute, **alt=""**. In this example, the attribute is empty. There is nothing between the quotes. This provides no value at all, because no description is provided to the search engines or the user's browser. A better example, would be to have a couple words to explain the image. Here the attribute says, "golf clubs":

```
<img src="golf-clubs.jpg" alt="golf clubs">
```

The best option is to be more descriptive, more specific:

```
<img src="golf-clubs.jpg" alt="My tournament winning
set of Callaway golf clubs">
```

What you want to avoid, even more than an empty alt attribute is an alt stuffed with keywords. This reduces the user experience, and Google might decide that your site is attempting to manipulate the search results with keyword spam. A spammy alt attribute might look like the one that follows.

```
<img src="golf-clubs.jpg" alt="golf clubs, my golf
clubs, buy golf clubs, new golf clubs, drivers,
irons, putters, woods, hybrid golf clubs, complete
sets of golf clubs">
```

Most websites have images embedded somewhere. As I have previously said, they are important for moving a visitor from attention through to action. In addition, there are a couple other ways that images play a significant role in the overall results you can achieve through your site.

One of those ways is by reducing the bounce rate of your site. The bounce rate is the percentage of visitors that come into a single page of your site and then leave without ever visiting another page. An embedded image can capture the attention of a visitor. That image can also be a link to another page. As the internet has become more image-based, users have become accustomed to clicking on images.

The whole idea behind Pinterest is related to sharing and clicking on images, so the idea has become mainstream. If you include images that are linked to another page within your site, and the visitor clicks, you have effectively reduced your site's bounce rate because this visitor did not bounce. Lower bounce rates are a good indicator that visitors are finding something relevant on your site. In other words, lower bounce rates are a positive factor with search engines.

Now think about this scenario. What if someone clicks on an image, and doing so takes them to a page dedicated to that image? This page provides a larger version of the image along with details about the image and other relevant content. You have grabbed that visitor and increased their engagement with your site because they were attracted to an image. In the process they may have made a micro-conversion toward your desired outcome. This dedicated page can lead them to the next step.

Furthermore, if you have created a page dedicated to a single image, you have created a page with great context for Google. From Google's perspective, that might make this into a good landing page, and worthy to be included in the general search results. Even if it doesn't make it to that level, Google will have a good picture (pun intended) of what this image is about. That allows them to give it more meaningful placement within Google Images.

As I have mentioned, Google Images allows an image search that anyone can use to look at photos and other images that Google has found. This extends the power of your images beyond the visual enhancement of your web pages. Each image has links back to the source. Therefore if you have interesting images on important topics that matter to searchers, you have another path to get visitors to your site. From this perspective your dedicated image pages do become landing pages.

Here is an example taken from a Google Images search. The image on the left is what shows up in the search. When I click, I see the image and the data shown here. Using arrows in the image, I have pointed out each link to the page where the image was found.

Video

Video builds on the thoughts presented in the images section. Google has a video search that looks for videos related to the search term. Google Videos is located at **video.google.com**. In this case a large portion of the results are videos from YouTube. On its own,

YouTube is one of the top search engines in the world, but since it is owned by Google, it greatly expands the search-master's power into the video world.

But Google Videos is not limited to YouTube. A general video search will include videos that are embedded into other websites. What that means is, if you have a video on your website, that video can show up in video search results even if you host the video yourself, outside of YouTube or any other video hosting provider. If Google has indexed a video from your site, in other words has included the video within their database, then the video search results can lead someone directly to the page on your site that contains the video.

If your video is hosted at YouTube, then the searcher will end up at YouTube instead of on your website. However, that can still be OK. Your business's YouTube video channel can lead the searchers to your website with the included URL.

The image below is part of a screen capture from a YouTube page.

The video itself, in this case, is right above the portion of the screen shown in this image. The page also extends below this snapshot. The important part is circled. This is the clickable URL that is shown to the viewer the entire time the video is playing and after. This becomes a source of additional traffic. If someone likes the video, and wants to learn more, they can click through to the website.

Any videos embedded on your website pages should be placed thoughtfully to help create a great user experience. Doing so gives your visitors good reason to stay on your website longer, learning more about your business, and building additional trust.

As you know by now, this book is about more than just making your site look good. It is also about making Google happy so that you get better placement in the search results. In Google's own words,

> *"Create a standalone landing page for each video, where you can gather all its related information. If you do this, be sure to provide unique information--such as descriptive titles and captions--on each page."*

What they mean here is that it can be more effective to give a video its own space, surrounded by information that matters most to the video watchers. By doing this, you may experience better results than just cramming a video into some small available space at the side of your page. But see how they also focused on "unique information such as descriptive titles." This takes us back to that important factor of uniqueness.

Google's recommendations then go on to say,

> *"Make it as easy as possible for users to find and play the videos on each landing page. The presence of a prominent, embedded video player using widely supported video formats can make your videos more attractive to users and easier for Google to index."*

Again, videos will stand out on a page if that page is created around the video rather than the video being forced into an existing slot. The most interesting statement in this sentence is "more attractive to users and easier for Google to index." If it's more attractive to users, you gain credibility and engagement. If it's easier for Google, you gain search ranking power!

CHAPTER 9 – KEY POINTS TO REMEMBER

Your use of color can increase or decrease the amount of time someone spends on your site. It can also influence their actions on your site.

Images can be effective at reducing your site's bounce rate. That is, if they are linked to another page, visitors may click and become more engaged with your site.

Videos can show in the search results and on the Google Videos site. Plus, when used well, they give visitors a reason to stay on your site longer.

CHAPTER 10
YOUR NEW BEST GUESS

You have been through each of the seven components of an effective website. Did you take action to make associated improvements in each of those areas? I hope so. If you did, it is likely you are already getting better results with your site. Remember when I previously said that your website was a guess when first published By executing on each of the seven components, even with uncertainty, you have improved upon that initial guess.

Now it is time to dig a little deeper, and take a critical look at your site. You are going to have the opportunity to grade your site from several different perspectives. The result of which will be further tuning of your site in a manner that helps it better comply with the types of sites that search engines like. At the same time your site becomes more goal oriented and effective for your visitors. Once again, it's a win for the search engines and for human experience.

This section will make the most sense if you have already implemented the changes suggested in Chapters 3-9, with some time having elapsed between those changes and now. However, if you made, or are making, a list of changes to present to your web developer, they may not have had a chance to make the changes yet, or perhaps you have not even provided them with the list. In that case, you will have to follow along here and envision the changes you have already suggested. Make additional notes relative to that perspective.

Website Grading

One of the problems that can occur after doing keyword research is that it becomes tempting to insert keywords everywhere. Indeed, this used to be a tactic that was recommended. The problem is that overuse of keyword phrases makes the text on a page sound unnatural to your human visitors. Doing so can also tip off the search engines that you are trying too hard to get their attention. It's a tactic that can backfire from a search engine optimization perspective.

So let's grade your website. Grab your red pen or marker, and ideally, a blue pen and a couple different colored highlighters. I'm going to start out by showing you a different way to look at your website, and then we're going to tear it apart!

The first thing you will do is print out a copy of your website home page. Eventually you can print out all the important pages, but just start with the home page.

Wait! Before you start, you have to look at your site differently than you have before. You are going to print only the text of your site. There are a few different ways you can accomplish this. My favorite method takes a look at the data as Google last saw it. In the Google search box, type in **cache:YourURL**, like this:

You will see the most recent version of the page that Google has in its cache. (In case you are not familiar with the term "cache" relative to websites, it is a data storage area that holds a recent copy of the real website.) At the top of the page there is a grayish box that looks like this:

This is Google's cache of http://www.chocolateuniversityonline.com/. It is a snapshot of the page as it appeared on Mar 22, 2015 19:21:46 GMT. The current page could have changed in the meantime. Learn more
Tip: To quickly find your search term on this page, press **Ctrl+F** or **⌘-F** (Mac) and use the find bar.

Text-only version

Take a look at the date that shows in the box. Is it recent? Does the view of the page below the box look like the current version of your site? If so, this method will work great for you. If not, you might want to wait a few days for Google to catch up with your most recent changes.

In the lower right corner of this gray box, there is a link that says, "Text-only version." Click on that. Now you will see the page with all images removed. If Google does not have a recent text version and you can't wait to get started, another way to get a view of the text on the page is to bring up your current web page, and select the content of the entire page. In some browsers you can right-click on the page and choose **select all**. Otherwise you can do this by scrolling to the bottom of the page, clicking your mouse in the lower right corner, and dragging back to the top left. Once everything on the page is selected, right-click somewhere in the selected region and choose **copy**. Then open a Windows Notepad or another basic text editor in whatever operating system you have. Paste your selection there. If you see images, find a more basic text editor. All you want to see is the text.

Now that you are seeing just the text of the page, the first thing for you to consider is whether that text does a good job explaining what your site is about?

If you cannot tell what your site is about when the images are removed, neither can the search engines.

Often times this quick view is very revealing. Suddenly the light bulb goes on and you say, "Wow, no wonder our site has never appeared in the search results. Google has no idea what we do." If your site fails at this level, then return to review the quantity and quality of text (Chapter 4), and make the improvements you need before continuing.

OK, you made it over the first hurdle. Now print out the text-only page in full so that you can mark it up. And get those pens, markers, and highlighters ready to go.

Test 1 – Excessive Keyword Usage

The first thing to look for is excessive keyword usage. It's good to have appropriate keywords in your text to tell Google what your site is about, but too much repetition is spam and can annoy your site visitors.

Take out one of your highlighters. Read through all the text on your printed page(s) and highlight your important keyword phrases, but not every one. Here are the rules for you to follow:

1. If the keyword helps someone figure out where they are, that they are on the right website, then do not highlight it.

2. If the keyword helps someone figure out what to do next, then do not highlight it.

3. If the keyword clearly helps your page accomplish its goal, then do not highlight it.

4. **If the keyword does not fit rules 1, 2 or 3, then highlight it!**

For example, if your business sells golf clubs then it would make sense to use the phrase "Awesome Selection of Golf Clubs" at the top to help someone realize they are in the right place. But then if you have text right below that says, "Click to see all of our golf clubs," and "here's what our customers are saying about our golf clubs," and the text associated with every image says "golf clubs" then you've taken it too far.

The site would be more friendly if it followed "Awesome Selection of Golf Clubs" with, "Click to see the best deals today" and "here's what our customers are saying." And the text associated with each image should indicate the attributes that make that photo unique, not the element that is the same. In other words, instead of repeating the phrase "golf clubs" with each image, you might have "Big Bertha Drivers," "Fairway Woods," "Hybrid Golf Clubs," etc. In this example, your "golf clubs" keyword phrase fits naturally into one of the descriptions, but not all of them.

By following the rules presented in this section you are highlighting each keyword phrase that is not necessary for your human viewers. If it's not necessary, then someone probably put it there because they believed it would be helpful for SEO.

Test 2 – Links on the Page

The second test looks at the links you have on this page. For this exercise, switch to a different colored highlighter. It will be helpful if you also have the regular view of your website showing in your browser at the same time you are going through the printout. If you are looking at the text version of your page from the Google cache, then links are underlined in blue or purple. If you pasted into Notepad or some other simple text editor, you will not see the links. You will have to compare the text against what you see on the main website to determine where the links are. Here are the rules this time:

1. Highlight the link if it is useless.
2. Highlight repetitive links that serve no added value.
3. Highlight any hidden links.

I will explain each of these points so that you can choose the proper links to highlight.

A **useless link** is a link that does not benefit your business or help the visitor take a step in the direction of a goal. For example, if you have a link to your web developer's site or web hosting provider's site, it doesn't help you. Plus there is a chance that this link will move your visitor away from your page to your web developer's site. Since that is not the goal of your page, this link is useless.

Repetitive links are not necessarily harmful, but they can be distracting. For example, if there are three phrases in the same paragraph that all link to the same page, you probably don't need all three links.

Here's a look at a section of text within a previous version of the Chocolate University Online home page. The first image below shows the actual appearance on the page. The second image shows the text version from Google's cache.

Looking for live, in-person, chocolate tastings? We recommend the Chocolate Professor website for chocolate, as well as chocolate and wine, tastings for in-home groups and corporate events.

Looking for live, in-person, chocolate tastings? We recommend the Chocolate Professor website for chocolate, as well as chocolate and wine, tastings for in-home groups and corporate events.

Both of the links, "chocolate tastings" and "Chocolate Professor website" go to the same page at **www.chocolateprofessor.com**. Is it necessary to have both links? Probably not, but it is a judgment call. Each link comes from a different perspective so it might be worth keeping both. I could keep "chocolate tastings" as a link because that describes what the user is interested in. I could keep "Chocolate Professor website" as a link because it describes exactly where the link goes. So I see value in each. But since they are so close together on the page, I could just as well decide to remove one. If I choose to keep the "Chocolate Professor website" link, then based on rule #2, I would highlight the "chocolate tastings" link.

On the other hand, you can see the following example has excessive linking. If each of these links goes to the same page it is quite distracting for the user without providing any additional value.

If this were the appearance of the real website, it would be a good idea to reduce the number of links. I would highlight each of the extra ones on the printout.

> Looking for live, in-person, chocolate tastings? We recommend the Chocolate Professor website for chocolate, as well as chocolate and wine, tastings for in-home groups and corporate events.

When I speak of **hidden links**, I mean links that you see printed on the text-only page, where that same link does not appear on the real website. That means the link will not be seen by your site visitors. If they don't see it, they won't click it. Perhaps this hidden link is an error and was meant to be a real link. If so, make a note to fix it. Otherwise, highlight it for removal.

Getting rid of hidden links is important because they can be viewed as a deceptive search engine optimization practice. Here is what Google says, "Hiding text or links in your content to manipulate Google's search rankings can be seen as deceptive and is a violation of Google's Webmaster Guidelines... When evaluating your site to see if it includes hidden text or links, look for anything that's not easily viewable by visitors of your site."

By removing the links you see on the text-only printout you eliminate the chance of being penalized by Google for a deceptive practice.

Test 3 – Missing Links

While hidden links are links that show on the text version, but are not apparent in the real site, missing links are the opposite. They show up on the regular view of your website, but do not show up on the text printout. These are links that exist as clickable graphic images on the website, but are not properly defined for usability and flow.

For this step you will have to review your main web page, and follow along on the printout. Here are the rules:

1. Start at the top left of your web page and work to the right and down. Look for every link and button and compare with your printout.
2. Every time you find a match, mark it with your blue pen.
3. If you find a clickable spot on your website that does not show on the printout, circle where it should be. Make note of what it should say. Most of the time it should match whatever appears on the screen.

Why is this important? From a search perspective you want all of your links defined. It helps establish the relevancy of each page. But it's also important for users. Some users may have text-based browsers or website readers. If they can't see the images, or the link cannot be read, because there is no text associated with a link, they won't know to click it.

Here's an example for you. These image blocks appear visibly on a web page.

The first says "click here," the second says, "read more." But when I look in the text only version, as shown to the right, I only see the "click here" link. "Read more" is a missing link. So I would circle that in blue on the printout.

> Over 20 secure unit sizes to choose from – regular & climate-controlled - $34/mo. & up. Click here »
>
> Penske truck & dolly rental, packing supplies, free pallets

The Final Grade

Now we get to the red pen. Go through your entire printout and put a check mark at each highlighted phrase, each highlighted link, and each blue circled area. Count up the check marks and write that number at the top of the first page of your printout. Put a minus sign in front of the number. Then circle the negative number as added emphasis.

How did you do? If you have a lot of check marks for the highlighted areas, odds are pretty good that you or someone else has tried to optimize this page in the past for search engines. The reality is that these keyword techniques and linking methods used to be recommended, but they no longer are. On top of that, when people are assigned to optimize a site, sometimes they add words and links just to feel as though they are accomplishing something. The point is that you have discovered some things that must be fixed, but that does not necessarily mean that someone did a poor job to begin with. Some of what you found may have been intentional, but it outlived its usefulness.

A number of the Google algorithm updates over the past years have attempted to purge search results of sites that are over-optimized. Google doesn't like being tricked. They want to present the best results for the searchers. While it is important to tell Google what your site is about and make it easy for them to understand, if you try too hard they might classify your site as lower quality, or even as "web spam." Then your ranks drop instead of go up.

Unfortunately, Google does not provide guidelines as to what constitutes over-optimization. That's why I have given you these rules for website grading to help you fix your site. If you fix the keyword usage and the linking, your site will be more friendly for your human visitors. At the same time, you are cleaning up issues that the search engines may see as deceptive and may be hurting your position in the search results. Following through on these steps can therefore help you with visibility, traffic, and conversion.

Now what actions do you take with this marked up printout?

Your next step is to look through your highlighted areas and see what can be changed. For keywords, are there some that you can eliminate? Or is there a better way to say something so that it makes more sense for your visitors or helps move them to your goals faster? Make note of any changes or ideas, and get these to your web developer.

For links, are there any that can be removed? Or, in the case of multiple text links in a paragraph, can you reword and change the linking structure so that it better helps someone move to the next step in your page goals? Decide what changes to make, and send these to your web developer. And, yes, you can even ask them to...

Remove the link to the web developer's website that they snuck in at the bottom of your site when you weren't watching!

There's no rule that says you have to keep that. (As a courtesy you might let them keep their name in place as a subtle advertisement if you wish.)

If you have many check marks for blue circles, then your website was created with a lot of thought to graphics, but not for search or usability. To resolve this, go back to the regular view of your website and identify which buttons or graphic areas must be fixed. Tell your website developer that all those spots need text in the "alt" attribute. Express what you would like the text to say in each case.

Now repeat this exercise with other important pages on your site, at least all the pages in the top level of your navigation structure and any pages you specifically want searchers to land on. Tell your web developer about all of these changes as well.

After the changes have been made, wait a few weeks. Then go back to the Google cache view, making sure that the date of the snapshot is more recent than the changes. Then repeat this exercise again. If the changes have been made as requested, your site should be in pretty good shape this time around.

Stealth With Your Competition

Back in Chapter 2, while doing research, you looked at the search results to see how deep the competition went for certain keyword phrases. Now that you have completed all the steps since that point, you can begin to analyze your competitors' sites. What are they doing better than you are?

Go through the Seven Components of an Effective Website to see how the top competitors in the search results appear. How well have they taken advantage of the basic SEO elements with their URL, title, meta description, and meta keywords?

How does the quantity and quality of their text look on their page? Using the Website Grading technique, you can take a look at their sites to understand their flow, along with what they do well and where they need improvement. **Those areas in which they don't do so well, are opportunities for you to do better, to surpass their results.**

Does their site answer the big three questions to help keep visitors on their pages? Can you tell if they have page goals? Do you see anything attempting to move a user from attention to action?

How about trust elements? Do they have testimonials, guarantees, visible contact information, and third-party validation? Does their overall visual engagement with colors, images, and video work for them?

If you see anything lacking on competitive sites, take advantage of it by making your site better in those areas. If they do something very well, use that to help generate new ideas of your own. With consistent attention, and constant improvement, especially the type you will see in the next chapter, your site will have the ability to overcome theirs.

CHAPTER 10 – KEY POINTS TO REMEMBER

View your site as text-only. If you cannot tell what your site is about when the images are gone, neither can the search engines.

Be sure that your use of keywords on a web page are natural and necessary.

Remove any links from your site that are useless, repetitive, or hidden. And fix any links that are missing.

You can repeat the lessons learned here on your competitors' websites to find ways to beat their search engine positioning.

The workbook will help you walk through each step of website grading. To stay on track, follow those steps now. If you don't have it, but would like the extra help provided by the workbook, get it here: **www.dominatethetop.com/workbook**.

CHAPTER 11
STOP GUESSING AND START KNOWING!

Now the game is about to change. Everything you have done up to this point has served to get your website back in the game. While each of the areas we looked at are important, the changes you made were still guesses. Yes, they should give better results because this time they are good, educated guesses.

If you want to carry the "educated guess" concept to the extreme, you could run some usability studies. Watch people using your website to see what they do and why they do it. Get feedback on different colors, layouts, wordings, etc. Most importantly, give the testers tasks to accomplish, and see if they can easily figure out how to complete those tasks. This activity can certainly help you identify more areas for improvement. If you find that people are stumbling through certain areas of your site or cannot figure out how to navigate to the places they want to go, then you have some real issues. Solve those issues.

At the same time, keep in mind that if you are getting opinions on aesthetic elements, most of the feedback you get will be personal opinion. For example, if you ask a group of people what they think of your page headline, you might get some good ideas, but you do not know if those ideas will appeal to your website-using audience.

Ideally, those involved in a usability study are going to look at how things work more than how they appear, because that's the primary reason to have a usability study. But along the way, it's not bad to get opinions. You can ask about specific elements such as, "should we have a video here," "would this image be better," etc.

Doing this will get you more information. The information can help improve upon your guess. But remember that your site will never please everyone. So how do you know if a change will simply please the individual present or if it will be good for your target masses?

I also want to point out that many of the things I have brought up in previous chapters revolve around good "rules of thumb." In general, a rule of thumb is a shortcut, something that has worked for someone else in the past. But the caution here is that "the rule" might not be appropriate in your case. It might be little more than a worthwhile suggestion. For example, back when I brought up the topic of color, I stated that "You might even discover that a page that is slightly more difficult to read might have an appeal with your target audience precisely because of the overall look of the page."

That's my point. The rule of thumb states that dark text on a light background is the winning combination. But that does not consider your industry and your potential audience. Someone searching for large manufacturing equipment will have different expectations from someone searching for a take-and-bake pizza versus someone looking for Halloween costumes. Even if it's the same person searching in all three cases, their expectations are different under each of these different conditions.

So, using that same topic of color, I concluded by saying, "Only testing can reveal this to be true or not." That's what this chapter is about, making changes that produce a real measurable difference in your results, regardless of what "rules of thumb" you might have previously accepted as true. This can only be accomplished with testing.

A Rule of Thumb might be a good starting point, but may not be appropriate in your case.

Do you know what a split test is? Sometimes it's called A/B testing. In essence it's a method of comparing two versions of something to see which gets better results. Even if you're not familiar with the name you might be well aware of the concept. You might recall from the preface that I was educated as a software engineer. My mind works to solve problems and create efficiencies. So I was contemplating and executing split tests well before I knew that's what I was really doing.

Here's an example from the offline world. If there were two places that I would drive between, I always wanted to know the fastest route. How could I determine that? Well, I could time my drive. One day I would go one way, and the next day I would go another. Whichever way was fastest wins. That's a split test, but that's a very simple version and is subject to errors. For example, what if it was raining one day, but not the next. Then I would be basing my results on the timing that occurred under different conditions.

So I figured out a way to improve results. When my wife and I each had to go from the same point A to point B and we had two different vehicles, she'll always go the habitual route. I would make a change. Perhaps I drove a completely different route. Or maybe I would just make a slight variation to the route. Since we were going at the same time we would both be subject to the same big-picture conditions. If it was bright and sunny, it was the same for both of us. Likewise if it was raining or a blizzard, we both had the same conditions.

In this case, most of the time we can conclude that whoever arrives at the destination first chose the better route. That was true as long as neither of us encountered something unusual, specific to a single route. What if one of us got stuck in traffic waiting for a train? This might be significant if we're driving the same route every day at the same time and there is always a train at that time, but if the train was just a chance encounter, then the experiment was invalid. We would have to repeat some other time.

Once we identified the faster route, our habit would change to use that route. But then I'd try another variation. Eventually we would discover the route that was best the vast majority of the time. That's how split testing works. Essentially you compare two things against each other, while trying to eliminate external variables, to see how the tested things impact the results on your goal. Ultimately we're going to look at applying this process to your website.

What is the goal of your business website? Get more leads, get your phone to ring, get sales? Split test it!

Basically, in the internet world, it works like this. You have two versions of a web page. One is your original page, your driving route habit, and the other has something on it changed, the new route. Whatever is changed is what is being tested. The purpose of the test is to reveal whether your original or the new version helps you achieve your goals better.

Just like in the driving example, you could run one page this week and the test page next week, but that might skew the results because of some big-picture environmental thing. Perhaps something on the news caused spending to tighten a little bit. So fewer people purchase the second week, but you think the drop was related to the new page. Therefore, it would be best to run both of the pages simultaneously so they are each impacted by any change in the online buying environment. Effectively, you want all external variables to create equal impact across the tests.

With computers running the test, one version of your pages can be assigned randomly to each visitor. If the pages were identical, you would expect the same conversion rate on each page, given enough time. (Like flipping a coin, you might not get the same number of heads as tails in 10 flips, but the more you flip the coin, the nearer heads and tails each approach 50%.) But now that the pages are different, any change in conversion rate can be attributed to the difference between pages, not any outside factors. Once you find a change that gets better results than the original, you keep the new version. Now do a new test to see if you can beat this one. See, no more guessing!

The easiest way to test a change is to make a duplicate of the page you wish to test. Most website development platforms will allow you to copy one page into a new name. Then you edit the copy to make the change you wish to test. Do not change the original. Do not add the new page to your site menu or link to it in any way.

Now that you have two versions of a page, Google makes split testing easy with a free tool for you to use, as long as you have a Google Analytics account. (If you don't have a Google Analytics account, go to **www.google.com/analytics**. There you will log in with the free Google account you set up earlier. Watch the video at **www.dominatethetop.com/bonus** to follow along to see how to set up the free account.)

I'm going to show you how to set up testing with Google Content Experiments. However, if you do not have the ability to implement the type of split-testing that Google or other services provide, I am including the link to a tool which you can use to determine split test results manually. Just go to **www.splittesttool.com**. I have created a video showing you how to use this tool. You can also get access to this bonus training video at **www.dominatethetop.com/bonus**.

Using Google Experiments

To begin a split testing experiment using Google's tools, sign in to your Google Analytics account. Assuming you see the **audience**

overview page of analytics, go down the left side to the **Behavior** menu item. (Previously, this was the Content menu. The name may have changed, but the position and function remains the same.) The correct item is circled on this image.

Once you have clicked on **Behavior**, choose **Experiments** near the bottom of the menu list. The resulting page will help you get started with your experiment and show existing experiments, if any. Click the **Create experiment** button near the top left.

At this point, the **Content Experiments - Create a new experiment** page will come up. Give your experiments a name. This name should be something meaningful to you that describes what you are doing. Then, pick an objective for the experiment. Initially the "select a metric" dropdown will contain Site Usage objectives.

Content Experiments - Create a new experiment

1 Choose an experiment objective

Name for this experiment

Untitled experiment

Objective for this experiment (?)

Select a metric ▼ - or - Create a new objective

Assuming your goal is to test the effectiveness of a visitor moving to the next step in your site flow or sales funnel, the best type of experiment to run is one that is triggered by the destination of your visitor. In other words, the test will randomly present each visitor with either the original or the new page. Whichever version produces a higher click-through rate to the destination will be deemed the winner.

This option is not part of the default set of available metrics, but is easy to set up.

Click on the **Create a new objective** link to the right of the **Select a metric** button.

Enter a name for this goal, choose the **Destination** option, and then click on **Next step**. Then you will enter the web page you want the visitor to get to. Use the page name or path, preceded by a slash, not the entire URL. (See the note below the input box regarding the address format.) Then click **Create goal**.

Unfortunately the process of creating the destination goal disrupts the process of creating an experiment. When you get to this point, click the **Reporting** link in the upper left. Now you will see your Experiment listed so you can click on it. Then, in the metrics dropdown you will see your new goal listed beneath Goal Set 1. Click on it, as shown on the next page.

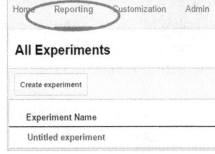

Next it asks for the percentage of traffic to use in the experiment. Whatever you choose here will be split between your original page and your test page or pages. For fastest results,

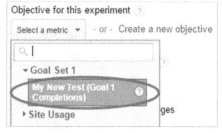

you would choose 100%. That means that half of your audience gets the original version while half of your audience gets the test version.

If, on the other hand, you are already getting good results and you think the new page is risky, then you might choose a lower percentage. For example, if you choose 50%, that means that half of your audience is treated as if there's no experiment going on, they go to the original page. The other 50% get divided between the test page and the original page. Effectively that means three-quarters of your visitors see the original, and only one quarter see the test page. Keep in mind that the lower the traffic to your site, and the lower your conversion rates, the longer an experiment will take to produce statistically relevant results. Running fewer than 100% of your visitors through the test will prolong the experiment even more.

The next selection is for email notification. If you want emails about the progress of your experiment, turn this on.

Then take a look at the advanced options. These are optional, and in most cases, adjustment is not necessary. The first item, **Distribute traffic evenly across all variations** is a relatively recent addition to this page. If you turn this feature on, you will get testing exactly as I described it above, with traffic given evenly to each page. The new default is off. In this state, the experiment is using additional math in an attempt to show the better performing page more frequently. The impact is that it can help you get to high confidence winning results faster.

Next, you can set the minimum amount of time you want the test to run. This only matters if you have sufficient traffic and conversion already happening. If so, you can pick a duration of shorter than two weeks. You cannot choose the maximum time because the experiment should run until Google can determine a clear winner at the confidence threshold set in the final option. However, Google does limit a test to 3 months if no winner is found.

The default confidence threshold is 95%, which is usually deemed as good enough. "Confidence threshold" is a phrase that defines the point at which you will accept one of the pages as being a winner. To put that into English, if you choose 95% it means that the experiment will run until Google is 95% confident that one of the pages is a winner.

When your test hits the confidence threshold, it means your results are statistically significant. It means that 95% of the time, the winner is truly the winner. Taking the more pessimistic view, it also means that 1 out of 20 experiments are wrong. Or, to put it another way, in 1 out of 20 experiments, if we let the test run a lot longer, we would see the results change. Since we want to get results in the shortest possible amount of time, 95% confidence is generally viewed as an acceptable risk. It takes much less time to determine the answer than using a higher confidence threshold.

To explain the error, go back to the car driving experiment. We could conclude that one route is faster because it happened to be better on two tests. However, maybe it's really only better 5 out of 100 times, and I happened to hit two of those 5 times right away. I conclude the route is better and stop testing even though I picked the wrong result. That can happen with split testing. But if you choose a 95% threshold, the wrong conclusion will only happen in approximately 1 out of 20 tests. As long as you continue testing other options, odds are that you'll eventually produce better results, compensating for any errors that occurred along the way.

However, if you don't want to make changes based on an error of 1 out of 20, then go with 99% confidence. That means you'll get the wrong answer only 1 out of 100 tests. Depending on your traffic though, this might take much longer. Google does not allow you to pick a number lower than 95% even if you are willing to tolerate more risk.

When you are satisfied with your selections, click **Next Step**. On the resulting page you will enter the URL of the original page and the URL of page Variation 1. Be sure your test page is already available and published on your website so that it has a unique URL. If you're not ready yet, just fill in what you can, and then click the **Save for Later** button. You can always come back to the experiment to complete the setup at a later time.

Below the URL for each page in the experiment, you can name each page. These names will show up in the report, so give them names that remind you which is which.

Underneath the name of the original page, there is a check-box called **Consolidate experiment for other content reports**. When you are first getting started with experiments, I would recommend that you check this box. If you want an explanation, hover your mouse over the question mark that Google has placed to the right.

Finally, there's a link called **Add Variation**. If you want to test three or more pages at the same time, you can do that. Google allows up to nine variations at once. This is a great feature, however, the more variations you test at once, the longer it will take to get to your chosen confidence threshold.

Click **Next Step**. If all is well you will see two green check marks on the page, along with a description of your experiment objective and small screen views of the pages that are being tested. The current page helps you set up the code for your experiment. You have a choice of manually inserting the code or sending the code to your web developer.

If you click the **Manually insert the code button**, Google presents you with a script that you can copy and then paste into your original page. (This also assumes that both pages already have the Google analytics tracking code installed. If that code is not installed, click the **Google analytics tracking code installed** link to find the appropriate tracking code.) If you can install the code right away, do that and then click **Next Step**, otherwise you can come back later.

If you click the **Send the code to webmaster** button, Google will present you with an email that is ready to send. All you have to do is put in the email address of your webmaster and click the send button below. At this point you will have to wait until your webmaster confirms that the changes are in place. When that is done, return to the experiment.

The last thing Google will do, after you or your webmaster have completed the code insertion, is to verify that it can find the code. Once the verification succeeds, click on the **Start Experiment** button.

Upon starting the experiment, Google's software takes over. There's nothing more for you to do except wait for the results to come in. You can visit the experiment at any time to see which page is winning. Google will present you with data relative to the type of goal it is tracking. For example, if you are looking at conversion rates on a page, you will see the number of visits to each page, the conversions, the conversion rate, how that compares to the original, and the probability of outperforming the original. The last column is the one to watch for the winner.

In the example below, the challenger has only an 8.3% chance of winning. In other words, the original has a 91.7% chance of winning. That's still below the 95% threshold, so the original has not yet been declared the winner.

Variation			Experiment Sessions	Conversions	Conversion Rate ↓	Compare to Original	Probability of Outperforming Original
☑	●	Original	121	26	21.49%	0%	0.0%
☑	●	Header and Quote	132	19	14.39%	▼ -33%	8.3%

Once a version hits 95%, your experiment will end with that version deemed victorious. Whichever one wins, becomes the new page on your site. It is the new "control" and is ready to face a new challenger.

One of the big benefits of split testing is that you no longer have to guess at changes to your site. Up to this point you have been getting more and more educated, you have seen the way people use your site, and your guesses are probably getting much better than they were originally. But with Split Testing, you don't just make a change, you make a test. The winner of the test always defines your next website improvement.

Now let me caution you about one thing. You just read that your new "control" page is ready to face a new challenger. That is exactly what it should do. Keep your site and your pages constantly evolving for better and better results. The temptation is to think that you just improved a page, so it's time to move to another page, or to stop testing altogether. Testing ought to continue.

There are more elements you can test. Perhaps you try a different headline, perhaps a new call to action, perhaps a link to a different part of your sales funnel. There are many things that can be tested to discover what best captures the conversion you wish to achieve. And you are not limited to one test at a time. Set up tests on several pages of your site at once. While you are testing a headline on your home page, you can test a photo on a product sales page.

Sometimes experiments will not produce a clear winner. It might be that there was not enough traffic, or that the conversion rates for both options were too small, or that both options were too similar. In these cases you can run a new experiment. You might try running a larger percentage of visitors through the experiment if you previously picked a number less than 100%. Or make the experimental changes more significant. Be bold and see what happens.

CHAPTER 11 – KEY POINTS TO REMEMBER

Web design rules of thumb might be good starting points, but may not be appropriate in your case.

Use split testing to determine whether changes to your web pages produce more conversion on your site.

Split testing gives you results based on actual conversions by real site visitors. This means you no longer have to guess what is best. Your audience effectively tells you by their actions.

Want more help with split tests? See the A/B Split Testing Tool training video at **www.dominatethetop.com/bonus**.

And go to your workbook! You will see many more screen shots so you can be comfortable that you are doing things correctly. (See **www.dominatethetop.com/workbook**.)

CHAPTER 12
FASTER WAYS TO THE TOP

Up to this point we have been looking at modifications to your own website. These modifications will help position your business at the top of the organic (unpaid) search results, and then convert that traffic into more leads and sales.

All of this is good stuff that will pay off for years to come. However, there is no guarantee that Google or any other search engine will put your site in the prominent position you're hoping for, or do it at a speed that you'd like. All you can do is give them what they want, keep giving them what they want, and then wait for the payoff.

Are you impatient, or do you want to jump-start the process? If so, you will enjoy this chapter. Here I am covering two additional methods to get your site positioned at the top of the search results. If you have already completed the previous steps then these additional methods will not only work fast, but can also be rather effective right away.

Google My Business

Over the years Google has worked diligently to improve the value of their search results. One area that was lacking in the early years was the ability for a searcher to find a business nearby that could solve their problem. In an effort to resolve this, Google began showing local search results along with the rest of the results on the page. Google Local was born in 2004 and quickly evolved.

The local information was shown as a block within the regular search results. But instead of just showing a title, description, and URL, the results included phone number, address, reviews, and other information.

Within a year Google created a free tool for businesses to add or update their business listings. If your business was already in Google's database you could update it with more accurate and useful information. And if your business was not present in the database, the tool allowed you to create a new local record.

The local offering continued to evolve into Google Maps, Google Places, Google Plus Local, and, most recently, Google My Business.

Cornerstone Plumbing, LLC www.cstoneplumbing.com 1 Google review · Google+ page	(A) 1305 Poplar Dr Waukesha, WI (262) 896-9006
Best Price Plumbing Inc www.bestpriceplumbing.com Google+ page	(B) 2315 Badger Dr Waukesha, WI (262) 547-1124
Cox Plumbing Co Inc coxplumbingco.com 2 Google reviews	(C) 616 E Broadway St Waukesha, WI (262) 542-6921
Urban's Plumbing www.urbansplumbing.com Google+ page	(D) Waukesha, WI (262) 894-9695
Midwest Plumbing midwest-plumbing.com Google+ page	(E) W246 S3150 Industrial Ln Waukesha, WI (262) 522-7494
Austin Plumbing Company www.smellgoodplumber.com Google+ page	(F) Waukesha, WI (262) 542-1999
Burton Plumbing Co. www.burtonplumbingco.com 1 Google review · Google+ page	(G) 1603 Square Cir Waukesha, WI (262) 786-3677

Within the search results, the appearance has also changed over time. Today, when I search for a single word, e.g. plumbing, the search results contain a local block that looks like the one you see on the opposite page.

There are seven local businesses with their name, website URL (if they have one of their own), a link to available reviews, and a link to their Google Plus page. Then to the right of each business you see a map pin letter followed by their physical address and phone number. These same map pin designations are shown in a map located to the upper right of the search results. This helps searchers find the closest business to fulfill their needs.

Map for plumbing

While there has been a bit of an identity crisis as to the naming of Google's local service, one consistent truth remains:

Managing your business records with Google's tools is the fastest way to get page 1 search results for free!

Therefore you must ensure that your business is properly listed. Take a few minutes to claim and update your listing if it exists, or create the listing if it does not.

If your business has a storefront, odds are good that you already have a Google My Business listing even if you never asked for it and even if you don't have a website. Starting with Google Local, Google attempted to identify businesses that serve a local community and created a page for each business they found. Even without a storefront, if your business has had a website with a physical address disclosed on the site, or the business appeared in some other directory, then it is likely that Google has created a page for your business as well.

By embedding this local information into the broader results, Google is helping to drive more business to those who are properly set up to take advantage of this. That's why you must make sure your business is correctly listed. This is an opportunity to get ahead of your competition in the results so you get more eyeballs on your business listing and more visitors to your website and walking through your doors.

Unless you manage your free Google page, you are allowing Google to use the data they believe to be true about your business. That data is not always accurate. For example, if the text on your website did not clearly identify your industry, Google might not display your business in the correct search results. They might associate your business with the wrong keywords. It's also possible that an address-error places your business in the wrong location on the map. That could be really confusing for potential prospects who might try to visit your store or office.

Since many businesses are not even aware that they have this free page available through Google, they are not managing their page. That means it is still quite easy to improve your results relative to your competition. With a little attention, your business can shoot to the top of the list and have a prominent first page search results position.

What's really interesting is that most people, when they see your local listing, will click on the title to go straight to your website. They don't even bother to look at the page that Google created and you modified. But by taking the time to modify the page, and including all the information that Google wants, you get preferential positioning in the results. It's a nice reward for a little work.

Furthermore, this page that Google created has evolved into Google's social sphere of Google Plus. So once you begin managing your business page, you can start including more social content such as updates about your business or links to your blog or links to other interesting business-related information. Doing this has the potential to create greater awareness and authority for your business within your marketplace. It's another way for your business to get found online.

Getting Started with Google My Business

How do you claim your Google My Business listing? First, note that if you have previously used Google Places for Business or the Google Plus Pages Dashboard for managing your business information, then your account has automatically been converted to Google My Business. If you have not used those older services, or you are unsure, the process is rather simple. Go through the instructions that follow.

Start at **www.google.com/business**. If you are redirected to a plus.google.com address, then you are already logged in and have a page with Google My Business. Otherwise you will see a page similar to the one shown below.

Click the **Get on Google** button. Google may prompt you to log in at that point. If you already have a Google account for Gmail or Google Analytics, use that one. Otherwise you can create a new Google Account.

Once you are logged in, you will see a map with a search box in the upper left. Type your business name and address in the box to search for your business. Several options may be shown. If your business is in the list, click on it. If it's not, click the item that says, "None of these match" to add your business. Continue to follow the instructions that appear. If your listing is new, you will complete the process after Google sends you a verification postcard. (Go to **www.dominatethetop.com/fast** for access to a training video that will walk you through the setup process.)

Once your listing is claimed, confirmed, and publicly available, make sure that the information remains accurate and up-to-date. Also encourage your customers to provide honest, unbiased reviews. Tell them to go to your Google page, and click the "write a review" button in the middle section of the page.

Google Adwords

While Google My Business provides the fastest free method to get first page search results, Google Adwords gives you the ability to instantly buy your way to the top. Adwords is a vast and powerful system for advertising your business in Google search results, as well as on many other websites around the internet.

There are several good books written on the subject of Google Adwords. If you want to master the subject you will have to go way beyond what I am going to introduce you to here. My purpose is not to give you expertise in Google Adwords, but rather make you aware of the potential for your business.

That said, it's also not necessary to master Adwords to get good results. You can get started, test it out, and then work to improve the impact for your business. If you decide that this form of paid advertising can work well for your business then go deeper, digging into some of the many resources that are available on this topic.

The key point is that some of the search results, at the top of nearly every search results page, are really small advertisements. Those businesses pay Google to be shown there. The good news is that you can do the same. Within just a few minutes you can open your wallet and pay Google to place your ad at, or near, the top of the search results for the keyword phrases that are most significant for your business.

You can get started with a very small budget. And, as long as you follow a few simple rules, you won't go broke experimenting with this type of advertising. But keep in mind that I'm just going over a few of the basics. I want to help you get started. As such we're only going to look at ads within the sponsored search area.

What is the sponsored search area? That's the top and/or right side of the search results page.

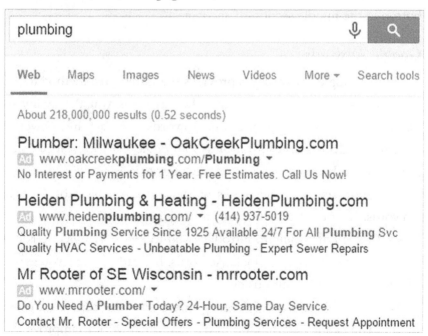

On the previous page I pasted a screen shot showing the top sponsored ads for the same plumbing search I presented a few pages back.

The owners of these three websites shown in the sponsored search results are all bidding to show up in this part of the search results page. Besides these top three positions there are more sponsored ads on the right side of the page. Google decides which ads appear in which position, and they will often move the ads around to see how well they perform.

Every time an ad is clicked the advertisers will pay a price up to their bid amount. There is no charge if an ad is seen but not clicked. In other words, impressions are free.

This is different from others types of advertising. If you pay for an ad on TV, on the radio, in a newspaper, in the yellow pages, or even on a billboard along side the road, you are paying for impressions. You are hoping that enough people see your ad and take action. With Google Adwords, you can choose pay only when someone clicks, and you set the maximum price you are willing to pay for that click in advance.

The maximum amount that you are willing to pay is one of the factors that determines where your ad will appear relative to the other ads.

There was a time that the top spot went to the highest bidder. That is no longer the case. While higher bids have a better shot at getting the top spots, the best performing ads are likely to be there more often.

Just like the regular search results, Google wants to deliver the best answer to a searcher's request. If an ad gets more clicks, even if the bid is lower, it's probably the better ad. Google makes more money by taking a little less money per click if they can get more clicks. They figure they are creating a win-win-win situation where the best ads serve the searcher, the businesses that created them, and Google.

Also refer back to the section on Google Quality Score. This scoring was created for their Adwords advertising. A higher quality score means you can save money on every click. A good quality ad that leads to a good landing page and a good visitor experience means that your cost of acquiring each a new customer goes down. And getting customers at a lower cost than your competition means more customer acquisition within the same budget. That can translate into big wins on the bottom line, helping you to consistently do better than your competition.

Smart Advertising Requires Math

Remember, nothing happens until someone clicks your link to visit your website. This is just as true with Adwords as it is with organic search. Just because impressions are free does not mean you want to get free impressions. It's not about the impressions. It's about the clicks.

Adwords is a form of direct response marketing. The purpose is to get your eager prospects to respond to your ad now, while they have their problem in mind. You want the searcher to take a measurable action.

In this case that measurable action starts with the click of your ad and then, ideally, continues with an appropriate response on your site. Therefore, before you create an ad, you must identify the action you want these prospects to take once they get to your site. And, I'm sorry to say it, but this is one area where math can make a big difference. When in doubt, choose an action that clearly leads to profit.

For example, let's say you have a product for which you have a $30 profit margin per sale. Let's also assume that for every 100 visits to your website, you make one sale. If you have to pay 50 cents per click then your cost of advertising is $50 per sale (100 visitors x 50 cents per click). That's $20 more than your profit margin. You just lost money. This advertising might not be a good idea unless you are confident in greater lifetime value of that customer.

However, this is not the end of the story. Like everything else, you have to test, measure, and modify. You can test the headline of the ad, the body of the ad, and various factors on the landing page of your website. What if you can move the conversion rate up to 4% instead of the initial 1%? And what if your Google quality score goes up enough that your cost per click drops to 40 cents?

These don't appear to be huge changes, but your cost per sale is now $10 (25 visitors x 40 cents per click). Subtract that from your $30 margin and you still have $20 profit. In this case you can throw as much money at the advertising as possible knowing that you're turning $10 into $20 like magic!

Keep in mind that the most important thing to making Adwords work for you is not the position of your ad in the search results, or even the number of clicks you get, but rather the conversion rate on your landing page. When your conversion rate is high enough, the rest of the math will work. And if your conversion rate is low or non-existent then no amount of advertising is going to help. This is why it's important to get your website in a reasonably good condition before paying for traffic.

How to Structure Your Ads

When you advertise with Adwords you set up your campaigns in a three level structure. At the top you have **Campaigns**. A campaign organizes around a specific theme or division of products.

Within each campaign you have a set of **Ad Groups**. Each ad group contains a set of **keywords** and a set of related **ads**. The ads themselves are the bottom level in this structure.

Back in Chapter 2 you started with keyword research. When you set up your ads you will want to use that research so that you are advertising to good words with commercial intent that properly identify searchers looking for what you have to offer. But you don't want to throw all of your keywords at a single group of ads.

The keywords and the ads must make sense with each other. For example, if you are advertising a plumbing business, one of your keyword phrases might be "fix toilet" but you might have an ad that advertises fixing broken pipes. These don't match. That's why you group keywords and matching ads into separate Ad Groups. All of the toilet fixing keyword phrases reveal toilet fixing ads, while the pipe fixing keywords reveal pipe fixing ads. By doing this organization you get higher quality scores, lower prices, and clicks that are more likely to turn into customers.

As another example, consider how you might structure a campaign for an Italian restaurant that advertises its delivery service.

Delivery service is only part of the offerings of this restaurant. So besides delivery they could have a completely separate campaign promoting their dine-in service, perhaps separating lunch from dinner or couples from families. As long as the divisions are designated by different sets of keywords and ads, good Ad Groups can be formed.

The diagram here shows a potential organization for this delivery service campaign. There are two Ad Groups. The first is for pizza, always popular for delivery. The second is for pasta, perhaps not nearly as popular, but still significant for this particular business. The keywords are associated with each ad separately

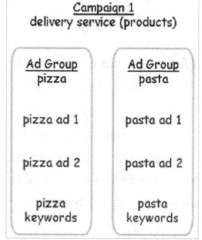

Campaign 1
delivery service (products)

Ad Group pizza	Ad Group pasta
pizza ad 1	pasta ad 1
pizza ad 2	pasta ad 2
pizza keywords	pasta keywords

because searchers are likely looking for pizza or pasta, not both together in a single search.

Setting Up an Adwords Account

To get started with Google Adwords go to the sign-in page at **www.google.com/adwords**. If you already have a Google account you can use it to log in. Otherwise you will choose the "Start now" button to create a new account.

Once you're logged in to your Adwords account, Google will walk you through the setup process. When you are first starting out there are a few points to be aware of.

First, when Google asks for a campaign type, change from the "search and display networks" default to "search network only." The reason is that the search network is the one that places text ads at the top and right side of the search results. The display network embeds ads (text or graphics) on other websites. While that can be a good idea and work well for some businesses, you should run display network ads as separate campaigns from search network ads. Don't mix the two types in a single campaign.

Second, your campaign defaults will initially target a relatively large region, such as the United States and Canada. If you only serve a local audience that's way too big. You can change the targeting to city, region, or even zip code. Adjust for whatever makes most sense to you, keeping in mind that if your budget is small, a smaller region might be a wiser choice.

Third, in your budgeting you can choose to let Google set your bids to maximize your clicks, or you can choose to set your own default bid. If you want total control, then I would recommend setting your own bid. You can start out low until you feel comfortable bidding higher.

Another bidding strategy is to let Google set the bids at first, until you see what level they are coming in at. Then you have some knowledge you were missing before and can decide to lock in a bid higher or lower than what Google has been using.

Yet another bidding strategy is to go high, knowing that you will only pay 1 cent more than the next highest bid. The advantage of coming right out of the gate with a high bid is that you will likely show up in a prominent position. If you get clicks early on, Google will believe that your ad's quality score is high. In this way the actual amount you pay can drop because you have a high-performing ad.

Pick a bidding style that suits your personality and needs. But keep an eye on the expenses and results to make sure that it is helping your business.

Regardless of your bidding philosophy, you get to create your own daily budget. This is your expense safety net. For a rough estimate, consider this as a total monthly budget divided by 30. (Google actually takes your daily budget times 30.4 to calculate the total monthly budget, so you can work with that number if you prefer greater accuracy.) Google may overspend your daily budget, by as much as 20% on any given day, but they will come in at or below the total for the month. For example, if you are willing to spend about $150 per month, then enter a budget of $5 per day. It's possible that you might spend $6 on some days and $4 on others.

Continue following the setup to create your first ad group and first ad. Google will walk you through each step of the process. When you finish you can still choose to pause the ad if you are not ready to start it running right away. If this is your first time ever creating a sponsored ad then take some time to feel comfortable before you say go.

While the first ad is paused, create a second ad that is similar (perhaps only changing the headline). Now you have two ads that will compete. Google will not show both ads at once, but rather one at a time. Effectively you are creating an A/B split test with your ads. Google will test the results for you and report what is happening.

When you are ready, start both ads and see what happens over the next few days. By default, Google will begin to show the winning ad more often than the losing ad. You can force them to be displayed evenly if you prefer.

Google shows how well each ad performs. That is, they show the number clicks and the number of times the ad was shown, impressions. Clicks divided by impressions is shown as a percent called CTR (click-through rate), which you can see as the middle column in the chart below.

Ad	Clicks	Impr.	CTR ↓	Avg. CPC	Cost	Avg. Pos.
Total - all campaign	51	1,857	2.75%	$0.22	$11.12	2.3
Become a Chocolate Expert I love chocolate and want to learn more with fun & easy weekly lessons www.ChocolateUniversityOnline.com	13	327	3.98%	$0.22	$2.91	2.5

This chart is quite compressed to make it fit on the page. I have removed several useful columns, as well as the competing ads, from this view. The columns that remain, shown to the right of CTR include the average cost per click (Avg CPC), the total cost during the advertising period (Cost), and the average position where Google placed the ad in the sponsored search section (Avg Pos).

As activity increases, you can see if any of your ads is a statistical winner. Go to **www.splittesttool.com** and compare clicks versus impressions.

CHAPTER 12– KEY POINTS TO REMEMBER

Many businesses are not aware that they have a free Google My Business web page. Therefore, one of the fastest ways to get on the first page of search results is to claim and update your business listing.

Google Adwords gives you the ability to instantly buy your way to the top of the search results pages.

If you choose to advertise online, send the traffic to a web page that has a good conversion rate. This way your advertising becomes profitable.

Choose a bidding philosophy that suits your personality and business needs.

Ready to implement Google My Business and Google Adwords? Go to the workbook now for extra help. (If you don't have it yet, you can get it here: **www.dominatethetop.com/workbook**.)

CHAPTER 13
OTHER CONSIDERATIONS

The seven components of an effective website are all items that are 100% within your own control. That's why those seven points make a good starting place. Get those right, and you are already miles ahead of your competition. But those are not the only factors you can or should influence.

In the previous chapter I showed you two ways to get to the top of the search results quickly, one for free and one with a cost. In this current chapter I will cover a few more ways to draw attention to your site. I am not covering any of these to the depth they deserve for full implementation. Yet, these are all issues that you must be aware of relative to your website's traffic and conversion.

Get Social!

Where to begin on this topic? I previously mentioned social media in the contact information section of the Trust Elements component, Chapter 8. That position in the book makes sense because social media offers a way for customers and prospects to reach out to your business. It's also a method that allows you to reach them. There is another important aspect of social media though. It's the new word-of-mouth. There can be complete conversations going on about your business even if you are not involved. Sometimes a business starts that conversation. Other times the conversation starts because a client is very happy and wants to share, or a client is quite disappointed and wants everyone to know.

It seems as though new social media systems come online every day! Which, if any of them, would make sense for your business? What's worthwhile, and what's just a waste of time? Sometimes it seems easier to ignore this entire subject.

I'm here to issue a warning. If you ignore social media, it's to your own business peril. While the previous sections of this book focused a lot on relevancy and uniqueness, social media plays big in the category of popularity. Google is starting to look at "social signals" to help determine search results. It not whether you have social media accounts that are important, but rather it's the interaction with those accounts. The Facebook Likes, Google Plus Ones, Twitter Retweets, and Local Reviews (whether 5 Star or 1 Star) can all impact the positioning of your website, both in the search results and in the minds of your prospects.

What's the best way to attack social media? My first answer is that you should use them all well, and get everyone in your company involved. To use them well, you must be social. This is a conversation, and you don't want to be that annoying person at the party who dominates the conversation. Instead, add value to the conversation. Interact with those who are in the conversation. In other words make sure no one is talking to the wall. And, then, when it makes sense, you can offer some of your products and services in a soft manner, never forgetting to be social and add value.

So that's the theoretically correct answer, but is it realistic for you and your organization? There's Facebook, Twitter, LinkedIn, Pinterest, YouTube, Tumblr, Instagram, and more. With all these options, and limited time, is it realistic to use them all? Perhaps not. Even if you eventually use them all, it likely does not make sense to jump into all of them simultaneously. It's better to do well with one than poorly with many.

Therefore, where do you start? I have two answers to this question. Both are logical. The first, is that if you already know which one has the greatest interaction with your target market, that's where you want to be. Set yourself up where you're most likely to find new business. The second answer is the default, and is very simple. Go where the most people are... right now that is Facebook.

For your reading pleasure and to guarantee that the information in this book becomes obsolete, here are some of the top social media (and related) networks with their number of users as of March 2015:

- Facebook – 1.415 billion
- YouTube – 1 billion
- LinkedIn – 347 million
- Google+ – 300 million
- Instagram – 300 million
- Twitter – 288 million
- Tumblr – 230 million
- Pinterest – 70 million

No matter which direction you go, there are some things to keep in mind regarding social media. While the emphasis is "social," the fact is that it's another form of media. Therefore the rules of marketing still apply. You need a target market and an offer for that market. And, since all media work best together, you will likely use social media to bring prospects to your website. That's why we started with the focus on your website.

When visitors arrive from your social media you want them to land on a page that is meaningful for them. You want that page to guide them through AIDA and into your sales funnel to reach your goals. If your website is still in the first-best-guess phase, then what's going to convert your social presence into customers? Nothing. And that's how social media becomes a waste of time. If, on the other hand, you are guiding your social visitors into a funnel that converts, you have a winning system.

Off-Site Linking (aka Backlinks)

One of the functions of the world wide web is that it is a web. It's a web of links, one site pointing to another site, pointing to another site. Search engines follow these links in an effort to catalog all the pages that are out there. In the process they can put together a picture of how your site fits into the bigger picture. What types of sites are linking to yours? What types of sites does your site link to? How popular are the sites that link to yours? What is the context in which the link to your site appears? The answers to these questions can influence the relevancy of your site for any particular search. And, depending on where one might find the links to your site and the context in which they are used, there might be a popularity impact as well. If your site is listed somewhere prominent, that can help your site stand out against others while simultaneously being positioned where your audience is looking.

Besides the link, and the context surrounding the link, there is also an element called the "anchor text" associated with your link. The anchor text are the words that appear within the hyperlink itself. For example, you might see a raw link on a page that shows up as the address, like this:

> For golf clubs click here: http://www.yoursite.com.

Google will understand this as a direct link to the website. Or, you might see a link with generic anchor text, such as:

> For golf clubs click here.

In this example, the words "click here" will take you to the same website as the first example. Those words have no useful meaning to the search engines, but the context around it does. The sentence itself reveals that clicking should take you to a site about golf clubs.

Finally, you might find a link that has specific anchor text, such as:

> Get new golf clubs today.

Here the anchor text of the link precisely describes what you will find on the resulting page. As a user you will expect to find new golf clubs. This is also very beneficial for search engines because no additional context is needed. This last example can provide the greatest level of relevance for search engines, though it may require a reader to think a little bit more than a link that says, "click here." Regarding links to your website, Google would expect to find all three kinds of links. That is the most natural.

Historically, the number of links to a page, often called "backlinks," has been a significant factor in the rankings of a site. You can consider a link to your site as a vote for your site. The more votes, the higher your site appears. Also, historically, the anchor text has been used to define significant search phrases that will trigger a site to appear in the search results. Therefore if your site has more links with the anchor text "new golf clubs" than any other, it has a good chance of ranking at the top for that particular search.

But I say historically because all of this has been changing over the years. Some of the more prominent Google updates have attempted to discover what links are natural versus what links are manipulated by the beneficiaries and search engine optimization professionals, what links are real and what links are "web spam." Often the way an average person links to someone else's site is with the URL or generic terms. The professionals more often use the specific anchor text.

If you consider that a link to a website constitutes a vote for that site, what would you want those votes to look like? As a consumer, would you prefer that each website owner is out there voting for his or her own site, such that the most prolific link-builder wins? Or would you prefer to have the happy customers voting by posting links within the context of a meaningful conversation? The former is manipulation. The latter is natural.

Of course, there is nothing wrong with trying to promote your own business, and that is done by providing links. Some of those links ought to contain quality anchor text to keep the relevancy high. And some of those links ought to contain your URL. But that's not all. With increasing socialization of the web, along with voice activated search on smart phones, it might even make sense to use natural conversational phrases as anchor text. What I mean by this is that traditionally we might have typed "new golf clubs" as a relevant search phrase, but "where can I get new golf clubs in milwaukee" is more natural in speech. Using the latter as anchor text may be increasingly beneficial.

There is a fine line between repeatedly voting for your own site and promoting your site to your potential audience. Google is trying to figure out where that line is.

You can take a cue from what Google says on the subject, "The best way to get other sites to create high-quality, relevant links to yours is to create unique, relevant content that can naturally gain popularity in the Internet community. Creating good content pays off: Links are usually editorial votes given by choice, and the more useful content you have, the greater the chances someone else will find that content valuable to their readers and link to it."

To simplify, if you want links to your site, create good content that others want to share and link to.

Blogging

Back when blogging was first becoming all the rage, I thought it was stupid, at least from a business perspective. After all, who wants to read the ongoing ramblings of a business in a self-promotional mode? I had to change my perspective when I saw who really noticed blogs... It was Google.

Blogging produced a more-or-less standard type of website structure that could be easily read, and contained enough textual information that it could be easily understood by search engines. Not only that, but blogs were often updated frequently, at least relative to the frequency of updates of corporate websites. This made their content fresh. Since Google could see unique information, relevant to various searches, and it had the freshness that searchers desired, blogs started hitting the search results in high numbers.

At this point, I recommend that every business have a blog. If your current website can support a blog, get it started. If it cannot support one, start a new website to contain the blog. I don't mean replace your existing site, rather create an additional one. There is no rule that says a business cannot have more than one website. Blogging is a key part of a strong visibility and traffic generation strategy that every business can use whether through a single site or multiple sites.

If you have gone through the effort of keyword research, you have a good idea of what phrases you need to use to capture your target market. What would happen if you created a brand new blog website that focused on a single cluster of phrases? In other words, if there are several highly-related keyword phrases, could you build a new website (or add blog pages to your existing site) designed to satisfy the needs of the searchers looking for those phrases? The goal you set for this new blog might be to move the visitors to the existing pages of your corporate site. Therefore a micro-conversion happens when they click from your blog to your static pages.

You ought to regularly post on this blog with information that the searchers seek. You can also write information that satisfies some of the searchers who don't yet have commercial intent. And you can provide highly specific details in some articles that would capture the attention of those who are looking for a solution right now.

Every time you reference something on the existing pages of your corporate website, you are creating a backlink to that content. Now you have a new method of voting for your own content, but you are doing it in a natural, highly leveraged, high value-added way that serves your prospects.

Plus your blog makes a natural entry into social media. Your blog is a more social version of your corporate site. As you engage users in conversation on any social platform, you can reference articles that you have posted on your blog that might answer their questions or provide them with more information on a topic of interest. This becomes a much softer sell for your business.

One of the obstacles businesses face is coming up with topics for their blogs. If you are already working a social media presence, you can pay attention to the topics that are being discussed. (Or, if you're not using social media for your business, watch the topics discussed on a competitor's social page.) These topics are important for your target audience. If the topics are important and prospects are looking for answers, these are topics that make great blog posts. You get to showcase your expertise, and Google puts it in front of searchers.

For extra help see **www.dominatethetop.com/bonus**. As a bonus, I am including a blog planning guide to help you out.

Building a List

Social media interaction, off-site linking, and blogging are all methods designed to increase the visibility of your business and translate that into more traffic to your website. At the same time, you may see a bump in conversions because of the additional trust that "being out there" and interacting with your audience provides. But primarily these methods are simply meant to move more traffic to your site.

Once the visitors arrive at your site, there is another factor that you must consider. Yes, unlike the other parts of this chapter, it's in the category of conversion. You see, now that you have your site in good condition and you are walking the visitors through your page goals, effectively using AIDA, and they are making the desired micro-conversions, your conversion rate is higher than it has ever been. But what is that conversion rate? Out of 100 visitors how many are taking action? Let's say for a moment that you have done good enough to have established a 25% conversion rate. Depending on your goals that may mean that 25% are purchasing, or it could mean that 25% are picking up the phone to call you. Even though either of these might be awesome for your business, it also means that 75% of your visitors are leaving your site without taking the desired step.

What do you do about that 75%? Or, more realistically, what do you do with the 95% or more that fail to take action? Or, to generalize, what do you do with the unconverted masses, regardless of percentage, who visit your site? You don't know who they are. You cannot reach them again. They will only return if they bookmarked your site or they do a similar search in the future and are reminded to come back, either accidentally or because you retargeted them with advertising. (Retargeting, sometimes called remarketing, is a way of showing your ads to people who have previously visited your website, in an effort to bring them back. Retargeting can be an excellent approach, especially when combined with what I'm about to say.)

To get around that loss, your site must have one more goal. It must make an attempt to get visitors to identify themselves. The problem is that people are not so willing to provide personal details.

They don't want to be bombarded by spam emails because they already receive enough junk. They are skeptical about giving away their contact information. This means that there are really only two conditions in which a visitor to your site will provide their email address. The first is that they already trust you. In this case, they are providing their email address because of previous experience or relationship. The second condition in which someone will provide their address is when you offer a reasonable incentive, an ethical bribe.

You have to make an offer they can't refuse. This is why it makes sense to give stuff away. Often the least expensive thing you can provide is information. That's because you can create it once, and give it away many times. You have to craft an offer, using the same rules of AIDA, to lead your visitors to take action, to desire this information. Therefore you make an offer that is irresistible to your target audience and the problem that is already on their mind. Targeted how-to information can work well. For example, "10 Things You Must Know Before Selling Your House" or "The Secret to Flying First Class for Free" or "Avoid the Puppy Training Mistakes that Will Mess Up Your Dog and Your Furniture."

After building up anticipation for the information you are willing to give away, you don't simply provide a link for visitors to download a report. No, you present this report in exchange for their email address or possibly for their name and email address.

The moment someone says "yes" to an offer, they are saying "yes" to your business. It's a tiny "yes" at this point, but it's still moving in the right direction. They are taking a small step toward your business. Instead of being anonymous visitors, they have identified themselves as prospects. They have identified themselves as somewhat interested in what you have to offer. Now if you can take that interest and immediately provide an irresistible low-price offer, you can quickly move someone from prospect to buyer. Of course if someone buys from your business and has a good experience, even if the price is low, the odds of them buying again go way up.

Even if you cannot make a low-price offer, or the recently identified prospect fails to purchase, you have still gained the ability to follow up because you now have this person on your mailing list. You are no longer dependent upon Google, or any other search engine or social media, to reach this individual. You can send an email with any offer at any time. Therefore their potential to purchase from you has gone up, and the cost to bring them back to your site has gone down. That's a big win for your business. Also, besides providing good, valuable information, your report can help prepare the reader to buy from your business. It can help set expectations so that they become a customer through a path that makes sense to you.

> *"Businesses must have the intention to build a*
> *list."*
> *--Ken McCarthy*

Keep in mind that there are several steps on the way from prospect to customer. The way you communicate with someone at each of these points should be different. When someone is on your prospect list, your goal is to help them make a first purchase. You must interact with prospects at that level. Continue to provide information and give them what they need, encouraging them to take that first step.

Once someone does take that step, then he is no longer a prospect. His email address ought to be moved from the prospect list to the buyer mailing list because he has become willing to try a product or service that your business offers.

I don't know about you, but after I have made a purchase with a business, I find it somewhat annoying to continue getting emails that are trying to sell me that first thing. The words are wrong, talking to me at too low a level.

Be courteous and move buyers to the proper list so that your message takes on the right tone. The reason is that when someone enters your buyer list, your goal shifts. At this point you want to strengthen the relationship to help the buyer return again for more.

A customer is someone who has tried out your products or services enough that they are happy to continue buying from your business. When someone gets to this point you ought to move their contact information to your customer mailing list. Here you might present some special perks that are only available to your loyal customers.

You might even start to segment your customer mailing list so that you can make offers that are even more targeted. For example, if your business sells golf equipment you might have a general customer list, but you might segment the list based on the brand of golf clubs your customer owns. This way when you have special deals, perhaps some branded clothing or an offer from the manufacturer, you can reach that part of your customer base first making them feel special.

Helping your customers feel special gets them talking about your business. This might happen via traditional word-of-mouth, or it might happen on Facebook or in some other online social setting. Either way, that's stronger social proof than you could ever put on your own website. Having your customers telling positive stories of their experience is the ultimate in driving traffic to your site. At the same time, it's a strong boost for conversion because the referred visitor is coming with preconceived expectations of goodwill and trust.

5 Things You Need To Automate Your List Building

There are five things you need to make your list building as easy as possible, so that it works 24x7 on autopilot. Those things are a quality offer/incentive, a landing page, an autoresponder, traffic sources, and follow-up emails. Let's quickly look at each of these.

A Quality Offer

This is your free gift or incentive that you immediately give to your new subscribers. It must be something of high perceived value so that your visitors are willing to pay the price of giving you their email address. You cannot build a list unless visitors are willing to opt in, and they are not going to opt in unless you are providing something they truly want, ideally that relates to the problem they are trying to solve.

Put some good thought, time, and effort into creating a worthwhile incentive. You might think it's free so it can be cheap, but remember the value you receive in being able to follow up with these prospects at any time. Each person added to your list is future potential income. Make your offer compelling, yet it should also be easy for your prospect to consume. In other words, what you offer should provide instant gratification. It should not require much time or deep thought for the recipients. You want them to be ready for more as soon as possible.

There are a variety of different types of incentives you can provide to the visitors who opt-in on your website. Some popular examples are a free report, a free ebook, a video, a case study, a free trial, a discount coupon, a limited access software application, and others. It really doesn't matter what type of business you are in. Giving an incentive for a lead is a good way to increase your number of prospects.

Landing Page

Sure, you can include a small form anywhere in your website, allowing visitors to opt in for the offer you make. It's a great idea to have these forms, but they will convert a relatively small percentage compared to a dedicated landing page. A landing page is more than just a form. It is a single page on your site that is designed to ask your visitor to take a single specific action.

The benefit of a dedicated landing page is one of focus. When you create this type of landing page, it is designed intentionally to limit options. The more limited the options, and the fewer the distractions, the less opportunity there is for your visitors to click away from the page. Data shows that a web page, tightly focused on obtaining the single desired behavior of opting in for a targeted offer, without the distractions of menus or links to other pages, creates the highest conversion rates possible. Keep this in mind when developing a landing page.

Within the context just defined, you have great deal of latitude. If you are asking for an email address in exchange for something free, you probably do not need the equivalent of a long sales letter. Often an enticing headline, some bullet points of what the visitor will receive, and a place for them to enter their email address is sufficient. A photo showing a physical version of what they will receive can also help, as can testimonials.

Be willing to test different versions of your landing page, and different components within your landing page, in an effort to maximize your conversion rates. Since this page is the point of entry into your email list, test continuously. As far as a starting point, the headline and details of the offer are good things to test right away.

Autoresponder

An autoresponder service allows you to collect email addresses automatically and add them to a list that allows you to follow up later. The ideal autoresponder service will allow you to send an email blast to the list at any time, a scheduled blast so you can queue an email in the future, and a sequential set of messages that go out automatically.

It's the sequential messaging that gives the autoresponder its first magic power. You can set up a sequence of messages in advance that will go to your new prospect, in predetermined order over a scheduled time frame. For example, when someone provides their email address to accept your free offer, the autoresponder immediately responds with an email delivering the requested product. But it doesn't stop there. Perhaps the next day, it automatically sends a follow-up to make sure that the prospect received the first message, and it welcomes the recipient to your company. Then the next day it provides additional good information. Maybe the day after that it makes another offer to the prospect, but this time the offer is not free.

You get the picture. With an autoresponder sequence you can set up your prospect onboarding process, delivering the experience you want them to have. Every new prospect gets the same messages, in the same order, on the same schedule, regardless of when they joined your list. It's all automatic.

The process becomes even more powerful if you divide users by interests. For example, if a new prospect takes up an offer that is in the second email, it may no longer make sense for them to remain on the original onboarding series. Because they took another action you know more about their interests. The autoresponder can automatically move them to the list created for those with this interest, or to a customer list if the offer was purchased. In this way your prospects and customers are segmented into mailings that make sense for where they are in your process.

Outside of programmed sequences, when you have a timely offer that you want to reach everyone at once, you use the email blasting capabilities. This way everyone on a list gets the same message at the same time, regardless of how long they have been on your list. You can easily deliver the same message to everyone on one or many lists simultaneously.

There are a variety of autoresponder services available. Many businesses seem to like Constant Contact because it integrates with some other popular business software, though it's a more expensive option when just starting out. Another company is Aweber. This is the service I have used for many years. Aweber is an excellent service with all of the features you would ever need. It has a good ongoing price point, offers a free trial, and has responsive tech support. A third option, which appears to have a pretty good following, is called GetResponse. And, finally, I will also mention Mail Chimp, which has improved its status over the past few years. For small lists that do not send very many emails each month the service starts out free with no time limits, clearly an incentive to get you hooked.

(Links for each of these autoresponder services, and any special deals they might have, are available on the book's resources page at **www.dominatethetop.com/resources.)**

Traffic Sources

If you have done the work presented in this book, you are already getting more traffic to your website. Within your site you can have instant sign-up forms with brief descriptions attempting to move visitors directly onto your mailing list. You can also have links within the context of your site or within special call-out boxes that will move visitors to your dedicated landing pages.

But just as important, now that you have an offer built into its own landing page, you can use different traffic sources to move people directly to the landing page. Besides organic search engine traffic, you can take advantage of social media traffic, video traffic (e.g. YouTube), paid traffic (search engine and/or social media), and even offline traffic. Anywhere that your target audience is spending their time is a suitable place to find potential traffic for your website.

Once you have a landing page you can be creative in where you find potential visitors. For example, right now I have a postal mail campaign that serves to get appointments so that I can help my prospects improve their online marketing. These appointments can lead to sales of my video training programs and do-it-for-you internet marketing services. Not every letter and follow-up phone call results in an appointment. So, at the back-end of the process, when it looks like the prospect is not interested, or we were not able to connect, then I give a link to a landing page as a thank-you offer for reading my letters and taking calls. This way I can identify those for whom the timing was wrong, but who truly can benefit from my offers. All these different media and potential traffic sources work together.

Ultimately you need to understand the value of a lead in your business. As long as you can acquire a lead, regardless of source, for less money than they are worth, you come out on the winning side of the equation.

When your business, or part of your business, operates online with a goal of completing a sale, there is another important number that you ought to know. It is called EPC, earnings per click. This is an important metric because it is an indicator of how well your product/service sales funnel converts clicks into sales.

To determine this, you have to have some performance numbers already, or make some good guesses based on what you already know. You need only three numbers: the profit on each unit of what you are selling, the net number of sales (after refunds, if any), and the total number of clicks. Here's the formula:

EPC = net profit times **# of sales** divided by **total clicks**

For example, say you are selling a $100 product and your net profit is $20 per sale. You achieve 50 sales in a week, and there were 500 clicks to your site. In this case the EPC would be $20 x 50 / 500. That's $1,000 / 500 = $2 EPC.

This means that every click to your site earns you $2. With this knowledge, you know that you can use Google Adwords or other traffic sources to buy traffic. As long as you spend less than $2 per click, you will be ahead of break-even. Understanding this number can open up many new traffic sources for your business.

Follow-up Emails

I gave an example of follow-up email services above in the autoresponder section. This follow-up is key to starting the new relationship properly. Keep in mind that when a new prospect enters your sales funnel by taking you up on an offer, they may not yet have built a lot of trust for you and your business. However, if you gave them something of value they begin to believe that you are an authority in your field because you're the one who put together this awesome incentive.

You must also realize that your prospect is warm at this moment. They have expressed interest your offer, and, by association, they have interest in your business, at least a little bit. So how are you going to follow up? What additional information can you provide over the next days or weeks to enhance the new relationship? How can you create more trust and more action?

Because your prospects responded to a specific offer, you already know something about them. Use that knowledge to help create a sequence of related emails. Make the content engaging so that your prospects feel connected. You can provide additional information that builds on your first offer. You can link to your social media or another page on your website. You can try to sell a related product. Decide on the experience you want your prospects to have and create a sequence to support that process. Decide how often your emails will go out and how long your mailing sequence will continue.

Finally, you have to actually write the emails. I find it helps to outline the entire sequence, then create the subject lines for each, and then write the individual messages. Finally, set them all aside. Come back with a fresh perspective a day or two later, and review the sequence. You might want to have others read through the series too.

Since emails are not always read as intended, you want to make sure that yours will be perceived properly before sending them out. Otherwise you might end up doing damage control, and that's not much fun.

With a good autoresponder service you will be able to see analytics related to each email. You will see how many of each message were sent, what percentage were opened, and what percentage of those were acted upon. If your open rates are too low, try changing the subject line. If your click-through rates are too low, make the message itself more compelling.

Whatever you do, don't forget to send messages. There is no value at all in an unused list. A hundred thousand email addresses does not help your business unless you have a relationship with the people on that list. You want that relationship to be strong enough, responsive enough, to take action when you email. And, by taking action, I don't mean thinking nice thoughts about you. I mean that a reasonable percentage of your list does exactly what you want them to do each time you send an email, especially each time you make a new offer with a product or service they can pay for.

By building an email list, and taking care of that list by communicating regularly with those on it, you gain a powerful and valuable tool for driving both traffic and conversion. Ken McCarthy, long-time copywriter, internet marketer, and founder of the System Club, once said, "Businesses must have the intention to build a list." He is correct in that statement, as list building and follow-up do not happen by accident. You cannot get the benefits without the effort. But the return on this investment is immense. Indeed, this may be the single-most important thing you can do for your website and your business. That's because this is not about ego and the desire to show up ahead of your competition in the search results. This is about actually making more money.

CHAPTER 13 – KEY POINTS TO REMEMBER

Start working with a single social media platform until you have a good presence. Then you can branch out to another.

Use your social media to drive traffic to your website and into a converting sales funnel. This way your social media becomes part of a profit-boosting system rather than a waste of time.

Links from other sites to your site are a good thing. If you want links to your site, create good content that others want to share and link to.

If your website can support a blog, get one started. If it cannot support a blog, create an additional site to host your blog.

Keep prospects, first-time buyers, and regular customers on different mailing lists, so you can continue to build the relationship in the most appropriate way.

You need 5 things to automate list building: a quality offer, a landing page, an autoresponder, traffic, and follow-up emails.

Building prospect and customer lists may be the single-most important thing you can do for your business.

You can use the workbook for extra help to get started with social media, backlinks, blogging, and list building. (If you don't have it, it's available at **www.dominatethetop.com/workbook**.)

CHAPTER 14
WHEN THINGS GO WRONG

Sometimes your site is invisible in the search results because at some point in time something went wrong. Sure, there are old tactics you, your web developer, or a hired SEO firm might have performed that caused problems for your site. But sometimes, things can happen that are completely unintentional. Sometimes a minor mistake is made that causes your site to vanish. This chapter is about some of these things and what you can do to fix them.

How Big is the Problem?

First, you must understand how big the problem is. If your site appears anywhere in the search results, then you can conclude that the search engine knows about one or more pages of your website. But if you can't find your site in the search results at all, even while intentionally keying in your business name and location, then something else might be going on. Therefore, before panic sets in, let's check to see how much of your website is in the search index.

This is a very simple search that works with Google, Bing, and Yahoo. In the search box, type **site:** followed immediately with your domain. It will look like this:

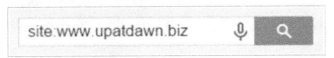

The results will show every indexed page, every page that Google knows about within your website. Ideally, you will see every page of your website. You might even find some old pages that you didn't know existed anymore. If they are no longer appropriate then you might want to create a 301 Redirect to point that address to a newer page. (Not sure what a 301 Redirect is? Don't worry, I'll explain this in more depth later in this chapter.)

Now take a look at the results of the site search. If there were no pages listed, continue following the "No Pages Listed in the Search Index" section below. If there were some pages shown, but some were missing, or you found old pages that are no longer needed, skip ahead to the section called "Site is Partially Listed in the Search Engines." Otherwise, if it appears that the site list is reasonably accurate, then you can jump ahead to "Other Issues that Impact Visibility and Traffic."

One other condition might exist, and that is you find pages that clearly do not belong in your site. You might find a few, or you might find many such pages. If so, this would be an indicator of a potential site hack, where the perpetrator created content to help boost their own results, not yours. The best thing to do in this case is to remove those disconnected, inappropriate pages, and change the hosting password.

No Pages Listed In the Search Index

If you find that the search engine does not have any of your pages listed (and your site is not brand new), then there are two big potential problems you should try to identify. Both of these problems revolve around the concept of "robots."

In this case, robots are not science-fiction machines that execute human requests. Rather a robot is a program that is designed to go out and explore the internet. Sometimes they are simply called bots or spiders or web crawlers. Each search engine has its own bots that attempt to follow links and crawl each page of the web.

Regarding the two big potential problems, the first has to do with providing improper information to the bots. The second comes into play if the bots never even get to your site.

Robots.txt File

Every website can have a file within the content of the site called robots.txt. This file tells the bots from Google and other search engines which files they are allowed to index and which ones they are not. Sometimes an error in creating or configuring this file creates a condition that prevents files of a website from being indexed. You can check to see if you have a robots.txt file for your website by typing **www.yourdomain.com/robots.txt** into your browser. (Of course, you will use your actual domain instead of yourdomain.com.)

The robots.txt file, if it exists, can contain several bits of information. Typically a file might look like this:

User-agent: *

Disallow: /

The first line, with an asterisk for User-agent, means that the information that follows applies to all robots that read this file. The second line, with a slash after Disallow, indicates that the visiting robot should stay away from all pages on the website. Therefore, if you want your site to be seen in the search results, you would never want a robots.txt file to look like the example above!

Instead, to allow access to all files within your site, the Disallow: should be followed by nothing at all. This is an example that gives complete access to your site:

User-agent: *

Disallow:

For most sites, this is exactly what your robots.txt file should look like.

Where the Disallow text becomes useful is when you want to prevent the search engine from adding specific parts of your website to their index. Let's say you have content on your site for employees only, and that content is within a folder called employees. You could block access with a Disallow like this:

Disallow: /employees/

With this disallow in the robots.txt file, none of the pages within the employees folder will appear in the search results. (Well-behaved search engines will honor this request. But this is not a security solution. The disallow request does not prevent access.)

You can have any number of separate disallow lines if you have a lot of content to block. Just be careful that you do not block content that you actually want to appear in the index.

A problem I have seen in the past, on a business website, is where the web host created a custom 404 error (that's what happens when a page is not found) that sent the contents of the home page. The logic was that if someone had a typo in the page address, the business did not want the person to see a page not found error message. They simply wanted the visitor to see the home page of the site as if they made no typing mistake at all. Makes sense.

The problem was that they did not create a robots.txt file. Normally when search engines look for a robots.txt file and it's not there, the website returns a 404 error and the search engine knows it's not there. But in this case, when search engines looked for the robots.txt file, it was not found, but the website did not return an error. It gave the contents of the home page instead. This confused the search engines because the home page HTML code is not a valid robots.txt file format. In this particular case their entire website disappeared from the search results. I caught the error when I tried to look at their robots.txt file and found that the home page came up instead. When I investigated further I found the configuration problem, created a valid robots.txt file, and all was well.

Google offers a robots.txt testing tool through their Webmaster Tools. Besides simply showing you the contents of your robots.txt file, the tool also allows you to enter the entire address of a page to check its status.

In the example that follows, the article called downtown-office is blocked because the robots.txt file is disallowing everything that starts with /down. The intent was to block the indexing of everything in the /downloads folder without making it obvious that there is a downloads folder. Unfortunately, this created a situation that is overly cautious and blocks other legitimate pages from ever making it into the search results. You can see the results in the following screen shot.

You can get more information about the robots.txt testing tool here: **support.google.com/webmasters/answer/6062598**.

Robots META Tag

Very similar in function to the robots.txt file, there is a way to include the robots data within any HTML document, in other words within the content of any page of your website. In this case you would use a robots meta tag. This tag provides instructions to the search engines for a single page.

Here is how one of these tags might look:

```
<meta name='robots' content='noindex,follow' />
```

In this example, there are two items in the content. The first says noindex. That is the directive to the search engines that this page should not be included in its index of searchable pages. This is a good idea for pages that are not meant for public consumption. For example, you don't want someone to click a link from Google search results and end up on your thank-you page, a page that is meant only for visitors who complete a specific action. That page should have a meta robots tag exactly like the example shown above.

Sometimes, especially with content management systems that generate the pages of your website automatically, a misconfiguration can cause the same tag as shown above to be placed on every page of your site. That would prevent your site from showing up in the search results.

A common example is a WordPress blog site. Within the Reading settings there is a check box for Search Engine Visibility. If that box is checked, then no pages within the site will show up in the search index. I have seen sites with this checked either by default or by accident. It doesn't really matter why or how this box got checked, the outcome is the same. Nothing appears in the search results and the owner of the site wonders why.

Search Engine Visibility	☑ Discourage search engines from indexing this site
	It is up to search engines to honor this request.

If you have a WordPress website that is meant for all to see, then verify that this box is not checked. Other content management systems may have a similar selection. This is an excellent choice to use while developing the site so that users do not find the pages before the site is ready. But you must remember to enable indexing when the site goes live!

For reference, the content portion of the robots meta tag should say "index, follow" for pages that you wish to appear in the search results.

Site Not Visited By Search Engines

Google and other search engines are constantly crawling the web to add content to their index. When the crawler encounters a new web address, it tags the URL for possible inclusion in the search index.

Normally you don't have to worry too much about your website getting found by the crawlers. As long as there is a link pointing to your site from another site, a crawler will discover the link, visit your site, and start the process of getting your site listed.

But if your site is brand new or you don't have any backlinks at this time, then it could be that your site doesn't show up because it is unknown, off the radar of the search engines.

In this case you can jump start the process by manually telling the search engines that your site exists. At this point, I recommend submitting to Google, Bing, and the Open Directory Project (owned by AOL) at the following URLs:

- **www.google.com/webmasters/tools/submit-url**
- **www.bing.com/toolbox/submit-site-url**
- **www.dmoz.org/docs/en/add.html**

Submitting your website at these sites does not assure you of inclusion in any index or directory. In fact, Google explicitly says, "We don't add all submitted URLs to our index, and we can't make predictions or guarantees about when or if submitted URLs will appear in our index." But experience shows that Google and Bing are pretty wide open to indexing new content. The Open Directory Project, on the other hand, is much more exclusive.

Site Is Partially Listed in the Search Engines

When you looked at Google to find your site listings, you might have discovered that some of your pages showed up, but others did not. The good news is that the search engine knows about your site. The bad news is that it didn't find everything.

The first thing to look at is the source code of one of the pages that is missing from the search results. Look at the code to see if there is a robots meta tag set to noindex. If there is a **noindex** setting, you'll have to get that changed to **index**. (For more information on this topic, refer back to the Robots META Tag discussion starting on page 167.)

If the page source looks good, then check the site's robots.txt file. (For more information on this topic, refer back to the Robots.txt File discussion beginning on page 165.) Verify that the particular web page of concern is not blocked by one of the disallow lines. As shown in the example on page 167, a single disallow line can block more than one potential file. For example, **Disallow: /abc** will block everything in the abc folder as well as any files that start with the letters abc. There have been several times over the years that I have unintentionally created similar errors myself.

Using a tool like Google's robots.txt testing tool can help you find the problem associated with any missing files.

Using a Sitemap.xml File

Besides errors in robots.txt or the robots meta tag, another way that pages of a website can be missing is that there is not a clear path to the pages. Generally if there is a good link on an existing page, either within your site or another site, the linked page will be indexed. If the linked page is new, it might take a while, but it will eventually show up. But if there is no good link, for example if the page stands alone, such as a separately designed landing page, then it becomes necessary to tell the search engines that the page exists and should be indexed.

A handy tool to help you do this is called a sitemap.xml file. A sitemap.xml file contains a list of every page within a website that you want indexed. In its simplest form, it can be a list of every file in the site, one per line. But a properly constructed sitemap.xml file will contain additional data. Typically it will show the file URL, the date and time it was last modified, how often the page changes, and a priority number as shown below.

```xml
<?xml version="1.0" encoding="UTF-8"?>
<urlset xmlns="http://www.sitemaps.org/schemas/sitemap/0.9">

    <url>
        <loc>http://www.chocolateuniversityonline.com/</loc>
        <lastmod>2015-02-07T10:57:00+00:00</lastmod>
        <changefreq>weekly</changefreq>
        <priority>1.0</priority>
    </url>

    <url>
        <loc>http://www.chocolateuniversityonline.com/chocolate-classes</loc>
        <lastmod>2015-01-26T09:55:00+00:00</lastmod>
        <changefreq>weekly</changefreq>
        <priority>0.9</priority>
    </url>

</urlset>
```

The priority number, between 0 and 1 (one example circled), allows you to tell the search engines which pages of your site are more important than others. This priority does not raise your pages above any other site, but rather tells the search engines the priority relative to other pages on your own site. This can help you tell the search engines which pages are more important than others to display. In other words, if Google decides it is going to show one of your pages in the third position of the search results, but it has two pages that it has to decide between, the priority lets you influence the results. Therefore, do not make the priority the same for every page.

In most cases it's more important to get someone to your home page and specific landing pages than to your frequently asked questions page. So decide on relative importance, and adjust accordingly.

Within Google Webmaster Tools, you can test your sitemap and/or submit it to Google so that it has this extra information about your site.

Broken Links

Sometimes a page you expect to see in the search results is missing because the links within your site are not pointing correctly to the page. Most of the time the pages that are listed within a website's menu will work well because those are obvious links to test. And if those links work then those pages will be added to search engines' index (assuming there is not a robots.txt or robots meta tag issue).

Missing pages are often lower-level pages that are reached through a single link on a specific page. If there is an error in the link, then there is no way to reach the intended page, for your site users and the search engines!

If you discover a single page missing from the search results, and you have already verified that the robots settings are correct, then look for all of the pages that are supposed to link to your missing page, and test those links. If the links result in a page not found error or take you to a different page, then you have found the problem. Correct the links and wait for the search engines to crawl your site again.

How do you prevent this type of problem from happening in the future? First you have to understand that there are two ways the problem could have come about in the first place. The first is due to insufficient testing of pages and links when the pages were built. That would be a development problem. But your developers might have successfully tested the site with everything working perfectly.

The second way the problem can appear is when someone changes the file name of an existing page. This can happen when someone attempts to optimize a website for search engines. They realize that a page could have a better, more relevant name, and so they change the name of the file, effectively changing the URL of the page.

This name changing problem can also happen quite innocently if someone discovers a typo in the original file name, for example if a product name was misspelled. So they correct the file name. If the website adjusts to those name changes dynamically, it's not a problem, but if the links to the page were manually entered somewhere, then those links will be broken when the name changes. The "Using 301 Redirects" section below shows you how to prevent this type of problem in the future.

Using 301 Redirects

A 301 redirect is a technical term that describes a very important action. When properly configured it is a response that a web server gives when someone, or something, requests access to a page that has moved. The 301 redirect tells the requester that the page has moved permanently to another address. If someone using their web browser tries to bring up a page and the server gives the browser a 301 redirect, then the user will not see an error message that the page is not found. Rather, they will automatically be directed to see the new page. For a human site visitor, the 301 redirect acts as if you are saying, "I want people who want page X to go to page Y instead."

Just as importantly, if the user is actually a search engine crawling the site, the 301 redirect tells it to update its database. Effectively you are telling the search engines, "Please replace page X with page Y in the results." Or another way to think of it, "Page Y is the new page X."

Here is what Google says about 301 redirects, "If you need to change the URL of a page as it is shown in search engine results, we recommend that you use a server-side 301 redirect. This is the best way to ensure that users and search engines are directed to the correct page."

What this means is that any time you change the name of an existing page, you ought to implement a 301 redirect from the old page name to the new page name. If you do this, you will never create broken links within your website. Simply assume that any page you have previously created is already known within your website and the search engines. It doesn't matter if you rename a page for SEO purposes, or to fix a typo, or for any other reason. If you create a 301 redirect no one gets lost. Users get the correct page, and search engines are updated. Of course it's still most desirable to fix the links within your website, but if you miss something it will still work.

So how do you implement 301 redirects? Often this is a little easier said than done. The answer really depends on how your website is coded and on what platform. Worst case scenario, if your website is pure HTML, you will have to contact your web hosting company to find out what they recommend. On the other hand, if your website was created using a programming language such as PHP or ASP.NET there are ways to program 301 redirects. In this case you will have to contact your website developer. If your website is hosted on a Linux server you may be able to add all redirects to a single file called .htaccess. This method is convenient because it keeps all of the redirects in one place. You can check with your web hosting company to ask about this.

If your website is created in WordPress then you can do everything yourself. You can install a plugin to manage the 301 redirects for you. For example, I often use the Simple 301 Redirects plugin. With this, you simply enter the old file name followed by the new address. Save the data, and it just works. In this case you do not need your web host nor your website developer to get involved. Other content management systems may have similar capabilities so be sure to search for other options.

Duplicate Content

If you have spent any time at all in the realm of search engine optimization over the past few years it is very likely you have heard the phrase, "duplicate content." Essentially, this means that identical or very similar content exists on more than one web page.

Why is this a problem? First, let's consider an extreme example to put it in perspective. This is the topic of uniqueness that I brought up way back in the Introduction. What if there were 1,000 identical web pages that could be brought up as the result of a search? What would Google display? If your business is designed to provide the best possible user experience, then showing 100 pages of identical search results is not a good idea. Therefore, most of those 1,000 pages are going to be dropped so that the first page of results gives sufficient variety.

Usually we don't find 1,000 identical web pages, but this example sets the stage. What if there are two identical web pages? Which of those two should be shown in the search results. Many businesses quite innocently end up with duplicate content on their websites.

A very common example occurs when a website answers to both www.yourdomain.com and yourdomain.com, without the www. That creates two complete identical websites. Both results can be crippled relative to how a unified website would appear in search. Test your own website with and without www to see what happens. Of course you want your website to appear in both cases because any particular user could attempt to load your site with or without www. But what you want is for your site to answer the same way no matter how the URL is entered. In other words, if you prefer to have the www in your address, the version of your site that does not have the www should 301 redirect to the www version. That solves this problem. You should also use Google Webmaster Tools to tell Google your preferred display method for the search results, with or without www, as shown here.

Site Settings

Preferred domain   ◌ Don't set a preferred domain
                         ◉ Display URLs as www.chocolateuniversityonline.com
                         ◌ Display URLs as chocolateuniversityonline.com

Another common example of duplicate content occurs on ecommerce websites. There are often several ways to view a product page. Depending on the ecommerce platform used, there may be different URLs, sometimes called dynamic URLs, or URLs with parameters added, that display the exact same content. You want this flexibility so that users can easily use your site, but which version of the page is the main version that should appear in the search results?

You can designate the preferred version with something called a "canonical URL." The canonical URL is a little snippet of HTML code that goes on each similar page to designate the single true representation that is suitable for the search engines. The format, as shown in the example below, is <link rel="canonical" href="the URL of the primary version">. This example shows a canonical URL for the home page of the site.

```
<link rel="canonical" href="http://www.chocolateuniversityonline.com/" />
```

The final example of duplicate content that I will mention is often seen on competing websites. In this scenario several businesses represent a common vendor, often a product distributor or manufacturer. When the resellers put information about the products on their websites, they use the exact product descriptions as provided by the vendor. The description is good and accurate, and the resellers don't have to take any time to modify it, so they don't. They cut and paste into their own website. The problem is that these potentially competing resellers have now created duplicate content. Which business will Google show in the search results? Or, if Google shows more than one, which one comes out on top?

You can come out on top, both in the search results and in the sales results, because I'm giving you the secret here... Let your competitors copy the information provided to them. From now on, you are going to improve upon the information. Rather than using the generic corporate-speak, rewrite the description in a customer-focused, more benefits-based language. And then include your personal experience or the experience of previous customers.

In the process, you will have generated greater, more content rich descriptions. Not only will your site stand out above the others in the search engines, but when a potential customer gets to your site, they will appreciate the extra information in their purchasing decision because you are giving information that your competitors are not! You win the uniqueness battle.

Other Issues That Impact Visibility and Traffic

Find problems with Webmaster Tools

I have already brought up Google Webmaster Tools several times. One of the reasons I refer to this, is that it contains a nice suite of tools to help diagnose problems.

In earlier pages I mentioned the importance of using unique titles and descriptions on each page of your website. Within Webmaster Tools, in the Search Appearance menu, there is an option to look at

HTML Improvements. This tool will show you pages that have problems with the titles and descriptions. It will point out where there are duplicates or missing titles and descriptions. It will also point out other problems such as titles being too long, too short, or not informative. For example:

HTML Improvements

Last updated Mar 26, 2015
Addressing the following may help your site's user experience and performance.

Meta description	Pages
We didn't detect any issues with the meta descriptions on your site.	

Title tag	Pages
Missing title tags	0
Duplicate title tags	11
Long title tags	0
Short title tags	0
Non-informative title tags	0

Note that these problems will not prevent your site from showing in the search results, but getting titles right can help you achieve higher rankings, and getting descriptions right can help get more clicks to your site.

Another problem area that the Webmaster Tools can help diagnose is broken links. These are links to pages on your site that don't exist. As I pointed out earlier, some may be due to page name changes or page removals, while others may be due to typos.

In the Crawl menu of Webmaster Tools, there is an item called Crawl Errors. In here there is a tab labeled as Not Found. This will identify all of the pages in your website that are linked to, but do not exist. Some bad pages are inevitable and will not harm your search engine ranking. But what you want to look for are the pages that should exist, or did exist, and were replaced.

Here's a good example from the Chocolate University Online website. About nine months ago we published a new version of the website. All of the pages in the blog got new URLs in the process. We created some 301 Redirect rules to resolve the majority, but there are a few lingering issues that would be nearly impossible to find without this tool from Google.

	Priority ▲	URL	Response Code	Detected
	1	chocolate-pictures/null	404	3/3/15
	2	chocolate-classes1.html	404	1/17/15

The circled item shows the page of concern. In the previous version of the website, this was a legitimate page that used to work. But now if someone goes to that page it generates a page not found error. I want to fix this. By clicking on the URL, a new window pops up which gives me some more details about the error. More importantly, it has a tab which shows me where the page is linked from.

Not found

URL: http://www.chocolateuniversityonline.com/chocolate-classes1.html ⬀

Error details	Linked from

http://supernova-11.blogspot.com/ ⬀

http://supernova-11.blogspot.com/2011/07/do-you-love-chocolate.html ⬀

http://supernova-11.blogspot.com/feeds/posts/default ⬀

In this case, I can see that the link is from an outside website. Someone must have liked the page and created a link to it within their own site. I don't want this to stop working. So I set up a 301 Redirect to fix the problem. If, instead of finding a backlink from another site, I found that the page was linked from another page within the Chocolate University Online website itself, then I would have fixed the source of the link.

The URL displayed at the top is the one that is not found. The three URLs at the bottom, are the pages that have links to the URL at the top. By clicking on the bottom addresses, a page opens in my browser where I can scroll down to see the actual link. After fixing the problem, I can simply click the Mark As Fixed button, and Google will remove the error from the list.

Conversion Problems

The previous issues pertain primarily to search rank and traffic. But before we leave the realm of problems, we should also look at a couple issues that have impact on conversion. We looked at customer focus earlier in the book because that's very important, and it's relatively easy to fix. Here I want to quickly look at the failure to get leads and the failure to complete sales.

First, I want to point out that your best weapon in solving these issues is testing. Run split tests in an effort to improve results. But where do you start?

Funnel Failure

One of the goals you may have for your website is to generate leads so that you can follow up, increasing the chance of making a future sale. Or you may have a complete sales funnel on your website, designed to capture the prospects' information and move them right into your sales process with the hope of creating an immediate sale. Either way, this sales funnel can break down in several places.

One of the most frequent problems is the failure to capture any leads. I brought up the topic of building lists back in Chapter 13. Remember, there are only two reasons someone will give you their email address. They either trust you, or you are offering a reasonable incentive, an offer they cannot refuse. (Please note that "sign up for our newsletter" is usually not a good offer. That's effectively saying, "Give us your email address so we can put more junk in your inbox.")

Now let's say you are attempting to build a list, and you are not getting any conversions, in other words no one is giving you their email address. The first thing you have to do is take a look at your offer and where you are presenting it. I have seen businesses make some nice offers, but they bury them way down on a page or hidden deeply within a website, as if they really do not want anyone to find it. Or perhaps they think it won't work anyway so they don't give the offer good positioning. If your offer is hidden, make it more prominent.

But if you have a good offer, and it's in a good position, without a lot of distractions around, and it's still not converting, then you have to look at the offer itself. Is this something that your visitors really want? How do you know they want it? If they do want it, then perhaps you are not explaining it clearly enough. Or maybe it's a great offer, but the context is wrong. Perhaps it is not solving the problem that is bringing those visitors to the page. I would suggest testing different wording of your offer, and a different layout, as well as different offers altogether. Keep testing until you find a combination that does convert.

Once you have visitors opting in to your offer, you are building a list of potential customers. This leads to the next potential failure point. You are getting prospects on your list, but nothing else. They take your awesome offer, and then they go no further. Again, there are several considerations here.

First, is conversion rate. At each point in your sales funnel, there is going to be drop-off. The biggest drop-off is generally between the point of free and the point of spending money. If 10 people have signed up for your free offer and none have taken the next step, it might be that the numbers are just too small at this point. If you have 1,000 people signed up and there has been no action, then there's a problem. But don't wait until you have 1,000 before you start testing. Elevating a prospect to a buyer requires another offer. Is the wording on this offer great? Is it easily understood? Do the prospects see the value?

And this leads to the second potential problem, does what you are trying to sell to the prospect connect with the problem they are trying to solve? You see, if they came to your website for a specific reason, and your initial free offer helped them out, connecting to their reason for being there, then it should also lead them closer to becoming a buyer. But that's only true if what you are trying to sell is also related to solving their problem.

Sometimes the easiest way to demonstrate something is to go to the absurd as a counter-example. It seems obvious that you would never give someone free money-making advice to get them on your mailing list, only to try selling them a swimming pool. The original offer and the second are completely unrelated. Sure, there are some people who would be interested in both, but this is not an effective way of generating swimming pool sales.

That's a silly example, but what are you offering to get the prospect, and what are you offering as the first potential sale? Does the first flow easily, without thought, to the second? If so, you've probably got a winner. If the first captures a large audience, and only a small subset of that would be interested in the next offer, then expect conversion rates to be very low. And if the first offer is only tangentially related to the second, then you need to rework the first offer, the second offer, or both. Make them fit.

For example, if the searcher came to your site for money-making advice and responded to your offer, then you might interest them in a related book, paid monthly newsletter, or financial consultation. Whereas if you really are trying to sell swimming pools, your initial prospect-generating offer could be something like "The Easy Way to Keep Your Pool Clean All Summer Long" or "How to Install a Swimming Pool and Preserve Your Property Value."

Shopping Cart Abandonment

I brought up the topic of shopping cart abandonment back in Chapter 8, Trust Elements. This is where someone is in the process of making a purchase on your website, but does not complete the purchase. I already mentioned that this is much more unusual in the physical world than online. People don't typically go shopping, fill up a cart, then push it off to the side and walk out of a store. Yet online, this happens all the time.

A 2012 study by WorldPay, based on answers from 19,000 consumers, revealed that the number one reason for shopping cart abandonment, a reason given by 56% of consumers, was that they were presented with unexpected costs. This is something that you can fix by openly presenting shipping and other potential costs up front.

At the same time consider the research by comScore in 2011 that states 61% of consumers are at least somewhat likely to cancel their entire purchase if free shipping is not offered. Shipping costs, and where you share that information, are certainly good items to test since they can have significant impact on abandonment.

The second reason for abandonment in the WorldPay study is also quite interesting. 37% of shoppers point out that they are just browsing. This is useful information because it presents a different behavior online versus offline. If someone is browsing in a physical store they are looking around, perhaps doing some research, gathering information, but they're not filling a cart. Yet in the online world, there is no extra work involved in adding to a cart. In this case, the shopping cart becomes the ideas cart, a collection containing items of interest without an intent to purchase.

I point this out because you should realize that some shopping cart abandonment happens because your visitors were just looking. They never intended to buy in the first place. So you don't have to worry about solving the entire abandonment issue. In some cases, your site provides the visitor with exactly what they want, the ability to dream a little bit, to shop without commitment. And someday, when they are ready to buy, they may be back.

Whether you are looking at funnel failure or shopping cart abandonment, you can use Google Analytics to measure the flow through your funnel at each step. This can help you identify where people drop out and, therefore, help you discover if there are rough spots in the process. By uncovering the specific areas where your visitors drop, you might find that there is a way to improve the process and better help your prospects become your customers. In this case you can view your efforts as customer service. Making your website easier to use benefits your visitors, and it benefits your bottom line.

CHAPTER 14 – KEY POINTS TO REMEMBER

If you are seeing none of your pages in the search index, check your Robots.txt file, your Robots META tags, and, if your site is new, submit your site to search engines.

If your site is only partially listed in the search engines, check your Robots.txt file, your Robots META tags, create a valid sitemap.xml file, fix broken links, and use 301 Redirects.

Use Google Webmaster Tools to see if Google reports any problems with your page titles and descriptions.

Use split testing to help resolve page conversion problems.

Use Google Analytics to discover places where you can improve conversions and reduce shopping cart abandonment.

CONCLUSION

Some Math You Will Love

Now before we finish up, I want to clarify something very important. I have two questions for you, and I'm pretty sure you'll know the answers.

1. Do you think it is easier to double the traffic to your site or to just get 50% more traffic?

2. Likewise, do you think it is easier to double your conversion rate or improve conversion by 50%?

Yes, I'm talking about math here, but this is simple stuff. It should make perfect sense that getting an extra 50% of your current traffic is easier than getting an extra 100%, and getting a 50% boost in conversion must be easier than getting a 100% boost in conversion. Certainly we'd love 100%, but I'm just talking about what is easier.

Now follow me here. Let's say you already get 1,000 visitors to your website each month. And let's say you convert 2% of them into quality leads. That means you get 20 good leads each month (1000 x 0.02). If you improve your traffic by 50% that would mean you get 1,500 visitors per month. This results in 30 good leads (1500 x 0.02). That's also a 50% improvement. That makes sense, right? Increase the input by 50% and the output also increases by 50%.

Of course if you keep the original 1,000 leads and improve conversion by 50% you would be converting 3.0% of your visitors. Again, that's 30 good leads (1000 x 0.03 = 30). Once again, you're increasing the input by 50% to get a 50% improvement in the output.

But we're not stopping there. No, this is where the magic is about to happen. You see, if we improve traffic by 50% AND we improve conversion by 50%, then we end up with 45 good leads (1500 x 0.03). That's an improvement of 125%!!! You get more than double the results by just improving traffic and conversion each by half. That means you get better results by doing two easier things than you would by trying to accomplish one difficult thing. It's like compound interest for your website!

Many people talk about wanting to get more and more traffic to their websites. And there's nothing wrong with that. But now you know that you don't have to work quite so hard on that, if you make good improvements to your site at the same time.

Implement the 7 Components of an Effective Website and do some testing to improve conversions. Add in some of the other considerations, especially list-building to identify and follow-up with prospects, and you are creating a winning combination.

Dominating Your Market

My final thoughts revolve around the original reason you may have picked up this book. That is, how you can dominate the top of the search results. But I will end with how your business can go way beyond that.

You have to be aware that Google does not reveal its search algorithm. It doesn't matter what I believe their algorithm is or does. It doesn't matter what anyone else believes either. Our beliefs do not make it true. There are people and businesses who have run comprehensive statistics to correlate various elements that have been discussed in this book, along with many other factors. These tests reveal interesting information that helps us understand what is going on at a particular point in time.

There are software tools available that allow you to compare your website against the first page search results for a particular phrase. These tools can be useful to help identify the elements that those sites have in common and rate your site relative to the same factors.

The assumption is that if you improve those particular elements (which can cross the lines of uniqueness, relevancy, and popularity) you will help your site compete favorably and have the greatest chance of rising to the first page results. There is clearly some logic to this. If the math is sound, and the proper elements have been identified, then this type of analysis can be quite beneficial. (On the resources page at **www.dominatethetop.com/resources**, I am giving you the link to one such tool.)

Of course, algorithms change. What is true at one point in time might not remain true forever. Even if you figure out Google today, the next animal in the Google Zoo might upset your plans. That's why it's important to be cautious when employing new tricks. If you get stuck changing the way you do business online every time Google releases a new algorithm update, you're going to be very frustrated. Stick to the fundamentals, do the things that Google encourages, and you can have your site rewarded for a long time to come.

The reward that Google provides is traffic to your site. But as you've seen, that's not the whole game. Your site has to convert that traffic into leads, and ultimately into sales, to be worthwhile. Working on both traffic and conversion can provide a boost to your bottom line. But sometimes, conversion can give a bigger boost. One reason for this, especially when you utilize paid advertising to get traffic, is that your advertising becomes more efficient. Advertising costs go up as you buy more traffic, but as conversion improves, your earnings per click goes up and you get more sales per advertising dollar. Therefore your cost of customer acquisition decreases.

Now you can look at this benefit in two different, but closely related ways. First, since your cost of customer acquisition dropped, that means more profit per customer and, therefore, more flexibility in your business. Second, with higher profit margins you could choose to spend more to generate new traffic. What I mean in this case is that you acquire the ability to outbid your competition. Since your EPC is higher, you can actually increase your traffic spend, paying more per visitor, because you know a higher percentage will buy from your website. Your deeper pockets allow you to pursue more traffic generation methods, which in turn allow you to capture a larger customer base. And now your competition looks at you and wonders why your business dominates the top!

ADDITIONAL RESOURCES

The practice of internet marketing is within a rapidly changing industry. I am providing you links to additional helpful content outside the context of this book. You can find this information at: **www.dominatethetop.com/resources**.

Furthermore, you can find me publishing content on two websites:

- **www.upatdawn.biz**
  This is a blog-style website with articles on internet marketing and other subjects that are helpful for business leaders.

- **www.24x7internetmarketing.com**
  This site provides internet marketing in the form of short training videos, most are 3 to 5 minutes long. Access to some videos are free. Members get access to all new videos, previous videos, and additional materials including transcripts and cheat sheets.

Both sites offer information about website visibility, driving traffic, and conversion.

SPECIAL FREE GIFTS FROM THE AUTHOR

Tools to Help You
Get Even More Out of This Book

As you read through this book, you have seen the following link several times. Here is the page, once again, where you can find the free bonus material: **www.dominatethetop.com/bonus**. Simply because you have a copy of this book, your FREE access includes:

- Google account setup video
- keyword research training video
- additional SEO topics
- advanced testimonials formula
- 8 features for high converting ecommerce sites
- split test tool training video
- blog planning guide

Here's the code you need to unlock the free gifts: **domtop1**

VIDEO TRAINING AND COACHING

No one cares more about your business more than you do. And since you made it through this book, you are obviously serious about improving your online business results. Congratulations on that! Most people never take the time to educate themselves in this way.

Yet, as internet usage continues to develop and change, success depends on continuous learning. You already have a website, you're taking the steps to improve it, and you have the commitment and determination to take the next step. That's why you're in the perfect position to expand the internet marketing know-how within your business. I have put together a program specifically designed for people like you who want greater visibility, leads, and sales.

This is a training and coaching system that includes a core library of 60 training videos and supplemental information. The concepts in this book are put on steroids, with additional winning topics added in, to boost your search engine results, deliver more traffic, and convert that traffic into more business.

While video is the core, many of the options provide direct coaching access to me. This way the lessons are customized for your exact, unique business needs. By taking this course, or assigning the responsibility to staff within your business, you develop internal expertise and drastically shorten your learning curve by several years. As a result, your business can dominate the top and stay there!

For details see **www.24x7internetmarketing.com/training**.

WANT IT ALL DONE FOR YOU?

Invariably when I bring up my training programs at an event, whether I am speaking or networking, someone asks if I can do the work for them. I strongly believe that we are at a point with internet technology that makes implementation easy when someone is properly guided in their actions. By acquiring the knowledge within your business, there can be ongoing activity and constant improvement to keep your business on top. This is the reason I wrote this book and put together the training and coaching program and many other supporting materials.

However, I understand that it makes sense for some businesses to hire out for these tasks. It may be more economical to pay for expertise, at least in the short term, than to take the time and effort to implement everything within your own business. Some businesses may also want the project kick-started, with the intent to take over a working system rather than starting from scratch.

Therefore I do take on clients from time to time. But before you go in this direction, I would want you to know that this is the right decision for you. To get more information and to start the process if desired, please visit: **www.24x7internetmarketing.com/doitforme**.

ABOUT THE AUTHOR

In 1991, Jeffrey Kirk stood in the central square of Kokshetau, Kazakhstan. At the front of a pressing crowd, he shook the hand of Mikhail Gorbachev, who would remain as leader of the USSR for a few more months. In retrospect, that handshake may have led to changes that circled the world.

The meaning of that trip, and several more to follow, changed the direction of Jeff's life as he began greater interaction with people of different cultures. This led to his forming an international trading business, the use of the internet as a competitive advantage in that business, and ultimately the formation of his own internet services company. Over the past 20 years Jeff has helped hundreds of businesses with their online presence.

Meanwhile, expanding cultural awareness propelled Jeff into refugee resettlement, where he and his wife have helped refugees from a variety of countries start new lives in the U.S. Having put together a successful resettlement program, and wanting to help more people, Jeff wrote his first book, titled *10 Million To 1: Refugee Resettlement – A How-To Guide*.

While writing that book, Jeff discovered that his magic power is the breaking down of complicated tasks into small, easy steps for others to follow. With this enlightenment, he turned the magic back into his world of internet technology and marketing, where he began training business people how to get the results they have always wanted with their websites.

When he has the chance to step away, Jeff enjoys traveling, bicycling, and playing Scrabble. He remains thankful to Gorby for the handshake.

Here are some places you can find Jeff online. Please **Like**, **Follow**, or **Connect** as appropriate!

- Facebook - **www.facebook.com/UpAtDawnLLC**
- Twitter – **www.twitter.com/upatdawnllc**
- LinkedIn - **www.linkedin.com/in/upatdawn**
- Google Plus - **plus.google.com/+UpatdawnBiz**

www.ingramcontent.com/pod-product-compliance
Lightning Source LLC
Chambersburg PA
CBHW071147050326
40689CB00011B/2013